# Paint
## effects
### manual

# Paint
## effects
## manual

### A step-by-step guide to creating faux finishes

**Kerry Skinner**

APPLE

A QUARTO BOOK

First published in the United Kingdom
by Apple Press
Sheridan House, 112–116a Western Road
Hove, East Sussex BN3 1DD

ISBN 1-84092-372-5

Conceived, designed and produced by
Quarto Publishing plc
The Old Brewery
6 Blundell Street
London N7 9BH

Art Editor and Designer  Michelle Stamp
Project Editor  Vicky Weber
Assistant Art Director  Penny Cobb
Text Editors  Claire Waite-Brown, Sarah Hoggett, Alice Tyler
Photographer  Tim France
Index and Glossary  Diana Le Core

Art Director  Moira Clinch
Publisher  Piers Spence

Manufactured in Singapore by Universal Graphic Pte Ltd
Printed in China by Midas Printing International Ltd

QUAR.PEB

9 8 7 6 5 4 3 2 1

# Contents

**Introduction**   **6**
Colour theory   8
Materials and equipment   16
Basic techniques   26

**Paint effects selector**   **35**

**The paint effects**   **41**

**Working with colour**   **42**
Using a sponge   44
Using a brush   54
Using a roller   64
Using a cloth   74

**Textured effects**   **84**
Stone effects   86
Leather and fabric effects   96
Plaster effects   106
Other textured effects   114

**Traditional effects**   **126**
Marbling   128
Wood effects   138
Other traditional effects   148

**Metallic effects**   **168**
Paints and powders   170
Metal leaf   190

**Patterns and motifs**   **210**
Stencils   212
Repeats   222
Other patterns and motifs   232

**Glossary**   **252**

**Index**   **254**

**Resources and acknowledgements**   **256**

Clockwise from top left: lilac colourwashed walls and
stone-effect fire surround with metallic-copper-effect
fireplace; kitchen cupboard with lining, collage and
decoupage; hand-painted, stencilled sisal rug and
decoupage screen; crackleglaze and decoupage
cupboard with gilded cornice.

# Introduction

The purpose of this book is to demonstrate some of the vast array of paint effects you can use to decorate surfaces. A paint-effects directory covers 100 faux finishes, all of which are clearly illustrated with step-by-step instructions, and cover a wide range of traditional and contemporary finishes with varying degrees of difficulty.

You will come to see that the most important ingredient needed for any project is enthusiasm and patience. A good general rule is to spend a lot of time visualising your goal – preparing, researching, and experimenting with colours and materials.

At this planning stage, samples and idea boards are invaluable. Often the simplest techniques and colour combinations can convey the most complex ideas. The biggest hurdle for most of us is learning to work confidently – gaining an understanding of your own intuitive response to colour is a great way to become more self-assured.

It is also very important to consider environmental issues – you need to find biodegradable materials and a low-waste technique that will make as little impact on the environment as possible. Most of the projects show the use of freely available multipurpose tools and equipment. Manufacturers are usually happy to hear your concerns and have begun to offer more choice for the discerning decorator who wishes, for example, to try out water-based products for a project when all traditional examples demonstrate the necessity of oil-based materials. Again, confidence and a willingness to experiment can lead to exciting results.

It is also important to realise that everyone has their own unique style and there is no definitive, prescribed way to achieve the perfect paint effect. The projects are offered as a starting point for each finish – to offer you help in accomplishing the particular painting you envisage. The techniques shown are open to endless variation and personal interpretation – and indeed your own decorative effects can add more individuality, glamour and surprise as well as being extremely challenging and fun to achieve. Let your imagination run riot and marvel at the results!

# Colour theory

Colour is amazingly expansive as a subject. Indeed, it is possible to become involved with colour and combinations of colour endlessly before even beginning to deal with the structural, textural or figurative elements of a project. This makes it necessary to have a focus and to ignore the dictates of fashion and fad that can distract you from your personal vision. If you have a complete understanding of the logic of colour theory you can choose colours to work with that could stimulate, soothe or enhance your enjoyment of home, work and life in general. Learning the simple rules means that you can then adapt, interpret and break them to suit your own aims.

The use of colour is a skill that needs to be learned like any other: an understanding of the colour wheel and its potential and values is essential, as is an appreciation of the relationship between colours and their combinations. As an element of form, colour is a major influence. It can arouse appreciation and stimulate more thoughts and feelings than any other aspect of interior design.

# The colour wheel

The colour wheel as a basic reference is an invaluable tool when learning about colour. The bands of colour – red, orange, yellow, green, blue and violet – are arranged in a segmented circle to show their relationships more effectively. Red, yellow and blue are known as the primary colours. Mix together two of the primary colours and you will create one of the secondary colours: red and yellow make orange, yellow and blue make green, and red and blue make violet.

primary colours

secondary colours

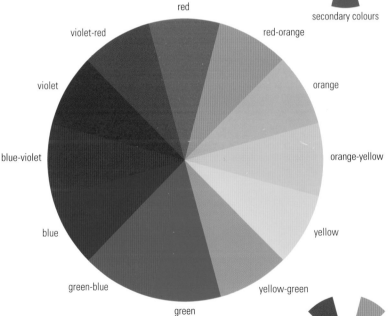

red

violet-red

red-orange

violet

orange

blue-violet

orange-yellow

blue

yellow

green-blue

yellow-green

green

Mixing equal parts of primary and adjacent secondary colours will produce tertiary colours. For example, red and violet make crimson, blue and green produce turquoise, and yellow and green create lime.

tertiary colours

All the colours on the colour wheel are hues.

Tints are created by adding white to a colour.

Shades are created by adding black to a colour.

Yellow has the brightest tone and violet the darkest.

# Hue, value and intensity

A particular colour can be defined by referring to its three qualities: hue, value and intensity. Hue is the specific spectral name of a colour, such as red, blue or yellow. The colour 'pink', for instance, is a 'red' hue.

Value refers to the darkness or lightness of the colour and includes tints, shades and tones. Tints are created by adding white and shades by adding black – although for a more subtle shading when mixing your own paint colours it is often better to use burnt umber rather than black. A sense of tone can easily be gained from the colour wheel, where yellow has the brightest tone and violet the darkest. Red and green, however, appear similar: they have a similar tonal value, which is why they can be mistaken as the same by someone with red/green colour blindness.

Intensity refers to the saturation of colour – its purity, brightness or dullness. A colour with high intensity is bright, strong and clean, as opposed to one that is muted, dirty or dull.

# Colour scheme considerations

When colour is used in a practical way, both the individual qualities of each colour and the relationship of combined colours need to be taken into account. The mood you create depends on the combinations.

Calm and restful schemes will be produced if analogous/adjacent hues on the colour wheel are used. This is because these colours are harmonious and close in character, as opposed to complementary colours, which sit opposite each other on the colour wheel. Combined complementary colours can be very busy and distracting. However, using a small amount of a contrasting colour within a single-colour scheme is a simple means of achieving an interesting balance.

Combining neutral tones, such as black and white, black and yellow, or blue and white, or clashing primaries against white will create a dramatic impact.

The positioning and amount used of each colour can suggest a colour is advancing or receding; bright, warm colours tend to advance while dull, cold colours recede.

Warm or cool colours can illicit an emotional response. Red is associated with passion, action and danger; orange with vibrancy and health; yellow with happiness, warmth and sunshine. By contrast, blues suggest space, coolness, tranquillity and melancholy. Our emotional response to different colours is also closely linked to their environmental associations. For example, green suggests growth and is refreshing and cooling. Brown suggests earthiness and harmony. Purple is the finite colour combining warmth and coldness, distance and closeness, and is often viewed as inspirational, religious and soothing.

Analogous hues on the colour wheel appear harmonious.

## External considerations

The balance of light, colours, tones and textures must be considered carefully in the planning of any project. For example, the textural finish of an applied colour will affect how it is viewed. A matt or rough surface will seem darker than a shiny, glossy one, due to the difference in reflected light. It is therefore important to have these practical considerations in mind when choosing the application of colour, in addition to the aesthetic, subjective reasons. Smooth finishes are more appropriate for utilitarian kitchens, whereas texture is probably better in an area where you want to suggest softness and comfort, such as in a reception room.

Complementary colours are opposite each other.

Combining complementary colours can be too intense.

Consideration must also be given to the source and the quality of light available. Daylight and artificial light affect colours very differently, so view paint samples in various conditions to see how the colour changes. Halogen bulbs issue a whiter light than ordinary household bulbs, while natural light varies with the seasons and all light is affected by the choice of curtains and lampshades. Metal, glass and mirrors can all be used to reflect and diffuse colours and light.

Warm colours advance while cool colours recede.

# Understanding paint

**Primary colour boards**

These mood boards demonstrate the different qualities of the primary colours, illustrating the huge range of intensities, hues and values within each one. They also clearly show how varied colours appear when applied to different surfaces and when combined with one another.

The application of paint is the quickest and easiest way to add colour to any environment. Paint contains two main ingredients: colour in the form of pigment and/or dye; and the medium that carries the colour, whether water, oil and/or a blend of synthetic resins and plastics. Manufactured binders make paints tough and easy to use, but their manufacture encourages the use of non-renewable resources. As the processes of decorative painting become demystified, the traditional techniques such as limewashing, distemper, colourwashing and simple plastering are becoming more widely used. It is hoped that more environmentally friendly products using organic pigments, binders and solvents will become more readily available.

## Mood/colour boards

When you are in the process of deciding on a scheme, it is a good idea to begin with a reference point. This could be a painting, postcard, photograph or a favourite object, colour or fabric swatch. Once you have gathered a number of reference materials, the best way to organise them is to create a mood or colour board. Combine all the elements you wish to work with on a large piece of thick paper or card. Try to keep the samples in proportion – so if you have a large area of flooring or if the wall effect will be a backdrop to smaller decorative items, aim to display the board with smaller pieces against the larger effect. Try out various sizes of pattern where possible – for example, by photocopying the originals at different scales.

It is important to assess each board against various light sources, to avoid any unnecessary surprises or disappointments. It is also recommended that you paint up a piece of board or lining paper with the same base colour and texture as the actual surface, then experiment with paint in washes, textures and depths of colour. Finally, view these samples in the light source you have decided on.

With such careful preparation and planning undertaken, when it comes to the real thing the work should be spontaneous and relaxed.

**Inspiration boards**

Each board has been put together to give some idea of the objects, samples and swatches that could be collected to inspire decorative projects. Many items, such as flowers, can also be colour photocopied to keep as reference or to cut out and use for decoupage. Some paint shops can take an item and scan it to obtain an exact paint colour for you to work with.

# Materials and equipment

Few mediums are more versatile than paint, but to take full advantage of it you need the correct tools and equipment, and some idea of how to use them. Don't splash out needlessly on tools – it is better to work with a few familiar ones than to assemble a large, costly collection that never gets used. Only a small number of specialist items are required to produce the paint effects that follow, and most of the materials are widely available in DIY stores or artist's supply shops.

## Paints, glazes and stainers

Paint is made up of three main ingredients: pigment, binder and a medium. The pigment provides colour and covering power; the binder causes adhesion to the surface; and the medium allows the application.

Today's paint is either water- or oil-based. Water-based products are preferable in many ways as they are non-toxic, odourless and environmentally safe (although they must be disposed of in accordance with local waste regulations). Oil paints, also known as alkyd paints, dry more slowly – a boon for beginners – and give a more durable finish.

A glaze is the transparent layer of colour used over a base coat. The general rule is: use a water-based glaze over a water-based base coat and an oil glaze over an alkyd base coat. The exception to this rule is that you can use an oil glaze over an emulsion base coat.

Colour stainer (or tinter) is a concentrated colouring agent. If you wish to use it for hand-painting, it must be mixed with a medium that has a built-in binder, such as a varnish, glazing liquid or artist's acrylic paint.

The list that follows describes some of the most commonly encountered types of paint. Remember that properties vary widely between makes. For best results always follow the manufacturer's instructions.

**Acrylic primer** is water based and used for sealing and covering wood and fiberboard surfaces.

**Oil-based undercoat** is an undercoat and primer combined, used before applying the base coat, especially on wood.

**Emulsion paint** is water based and available in matt (flat) and satin (mid-sheen) finishes.

**Stencil paint** is a water-based paint that generally flows better than emulsion paints, and is available in metallic and glitter colours. It can also be used as a stainer.

**Wood paint** is a matt, opaque paint specially formulated for wood. It is self-priming, has a high chalk and pigment content, and can also be diluted with water to create a wash for bare wood.

**Casein (or milk) paint** is a water-soluble paint with a soft finish similar to limewash that gives a 'dusty' appearance. Excellent for use on furniture and walls, it needs an additional coat if used in an exposed area. *See right* for recipe to make your own.

**Oil-based paint** comes in gloss, satin (mid-sheen), and eggshell (semi-matt) finishes. Gloss is used as a finishing coat on woodwork. Satin and eggshell are used on woodwork and can be used on walls wherever general wear and tear is likely. They are all wipeable.

**Acrylic eggshell paint** is a more user-friendly version of oil-based eggshell, with substantially less odour.

**Metallic paints** are widely available in tubes, pots and spray cans. New acrylic products are also available offering a range of iridescent, opalescent and interference colours. These offer unusual shimmering effects that are quite transparent.

**Colourwash** is a specially formulated, water-based, translucent, coloured glaze containing glycol retardants. *See right* for recipe to make your own.

**Matt emulsion glaze** is a water-based product used to thin colour and to act as a protective top-coat sealant.

**Acrylic glaze** is non-yellowing and water- and heat-resistant. It is tinted with acrylic colours for decorative glaze work. Water-based, it gives a short working time, about 15 to 30 minutes.

**Transparent oil glaze** is used for oil-based paint-effect glazing. It gives more working time but tends to yellow with age. Dilute with white spirit.

---

**MAKE YOUR OWN CASEIN PAINT**

- Mix 1 kg (2 lb) casein powder with 725 ml (1¼ pints) water in a container.
- Whisk to a thick paste and leave to stand for 30 minutes.
- Add a little liquid pigment and stir well.
- Continue adding pigment until the desired colour is achieved.
- Allow a little paint to dry to check its true colour.
- Leave the paint to stand until it has the consistency of light cream.
- Whisk again.

An infinite variety of opalescent, metallic and specialist paints and pigments is available.

**MAKE YOUR OWN COLOURWASH**

- Mix three parts liquid glaze (preferably matt) with one part water to the consistency of light cream.
- Tint as required.

Paint stainers are available in many different forms: 1 artist's oil paint; 2 pigment syringe; 3 water-based dye; 4 water-based stencil paint; 5 artist's acrylic paint; 6 powder pigment.

---

**MAKE YOUR OWN TEXTURED PAINT**

- Add approximately 1 part powder to 2 parts paint, plus a little water if the consistency is thicker than that of double cream.
- Allow a sample of the mix to dry to check its true colour.
- Always wear gloves when mixing and working with textured paint.

---

**Artist's oil paints** are used for tinting oil glazes for broken-colour work and oil-based marbling effects. You could use universal tinters as an environmentally friendly alternative to artist's oil paints.

**Universal stainer** or **univeral tinter** can be added to any paint or varnish. The strength of colour obtained will depend upon the medium being tinted and the amount of white within that medium. As a general rule, add the tinter a drop or two at a time, monitoring the results as you work.

# Textured paints and plasters

**Exterior house paint** comes in smooth or rough finishes and can be used for some plaster or stone effects.

**Textured wall finish** is available commercially and comes in powder form. It is a mix of quartz, clays and cellulose. It can be added to matt emulsion paint by the spoonful. *See left* for recipe to make your own.

**Decorator's plaster (gypsum)** is similar to plaster of paris, but has a slower drying time. It comes in pink and grey, as well as white which can be tinted with stainers or pigment.

**Alternative plasters** such as stucco or marmorino plaster are available for those with more specialist knowledge and an understanding of their application. The finish is harder and can be polished to give a smooth, soft gleam.

**Natural clay plasters** can be mixed with water into a workable consistency and will adhere to most surfaces if prepared properly. They are best used over a breathable surface.

# Specialist materials

**Metal leaf** is available in gold, silver, copper and a range of metal alloys or Dutch leaf (imitation gold or silver). Most metal leaf is available either loose or in transfer leaf form.

**Transfer leaf** is used for oil-gilding. Whilst easy to handle and cut owing to a waxed tissue backing paper, it may not retain the lustre of loose leaf.

**Loose leaf** was traditionally used for water-gilding as it can be burnished to a high sheen. It is slightly larger than transfer leaf, but it can be trickier to apply.

**Bronze and metallic powders** are made from metal alloys. Flakes of mica or celluloid can be used to create sparkle or lustre colours such as opalescent paint.

**Rabbit-skin (Gilding) size** is a specialist, water-based glue with a milky consistency. It is used in gilding and is available in powder, granular or sheet form. *See right* for recipe to prepare.

**Gesso** is used to create a smooth surface to take thin gold leaf. Traditionally it is made from a mix of rabbit-skin size and whiting. It can also be bought ready mixed. *See right* for recipe to make your own.

**Acrylic primer** offers a smooth surface as a gesso substitute if it is built up carefully and sanded regularly.

**Bole** is painted over gesso to add a sealing layer before size is applied to take metal leaf. It enriches the colour and makes a pliable cushion to assist the burnishing process. Bole can be bought as a paste suspended in water. A variety of colours are available for use with colored metal leaf. It is mixed with rabbit-skin size before use. *See right* for recipe to prepare, but always check the manufacturer's instructions as some brands may differ.

**Crackle medium** is one way of creating the effect of cracked, aged paint. Paint the base coat, followed by a coat of crackle medium. When dry, paint on a coat of the top colour (the heavier this coat is, the bigger the cracks will be). Cracking will occur due to a chemical reaction between the crackle medium and the top coat of paint. This can be used as an alternative to making your own crackle-effect paint system *(see pages 118–119)*.

**Craquelure varnish** is a two-part paint pack consisting of a slow-drying base coat and a brittle, quick-drying top coat. It produces an antiqued effect over painted surfaces. Rub artist's oil paint or coloured wax into the cracks for extra emphasis.

**Whiting** is a white chalk powder used in gilding and as a filler for pigment.

---

**TO PREPARE RABBIT-SKIN SIZE**

- Soak the size first in a little distilled water to soften.
- Add 10 parts distilled water to 1 part glue in a heatproof bowl over a saucepan of simmering water and stir. Do not let boil.
- Remove any scum that forms while continuing to stir.
- When the mixture is totally liquified it is ready to use.

**MAKE YOUR OWN GESSO**

- Make up 300 ml (½ pint) rabbit-skin size as above.
- Add 620 g (1 lb 6 oz) sieved whiting and stir gently until the mixture has the consistency of light cream.
- Keep the mixture warm, as it may start to gel as it cools.
- Do not allow to boil as bubbles will transfer to your work.

**TO PREPARE BOLE**

- Use 1 part bole to ¾ part prepared rabbit-skin size.
- Place the bole in a heatproof bowl over a saucepan of warm water, add a small amount of size and stir in well to disperse the paste.
- Add the rest of the size and continue to stir gently.

paint stripper, white spirit, methylated spirit, linseed oil and pure turpentine

adhesives for gluing fabric and paper, and sealing surfaces

waxes available include: 1 clear wax; 2 antiquing wax; 3 liming wax; 4 beeswax; 5 gilding wax

# Thinners, solvents and adhesives

Thinners are used to adjust the consistency and workability of your paint. Solvents are used primarily to clean and remove paint. Some thinners may also be solvents, and vice versa. Adhesives are used both for glueing and, in diluted form, for 'sizing' or sealing porous surfaces.

## Thinners and solvents

**For water-based and acrylic products:** use water for thinning and cleaning while wet. Check manufacturer's instructions for cleaning or removing when dry.

**For oil-based products:** use white spirit, linseed oil or pure turpentine for thinning; use white spirit or specialist brush cleaner for cleaning; use paint stripper for removing paint from surfaces.

**For shellac, knotting solution and enamel varnishes:** use methylated spirits to thin and clean.

## Adhesives

**PVA or white glue** is used in many paint effects – both as an adhesive and as a preparatory sealing coat for porous surfaces. It can also be mixed with powders to act as a binder or with paint or plasters to improve adhesion on surfaces.

**Spray adhesive,** available from art-supply stores, is an alternative (and less messy) means of sticking paper and other lightweight items to a surface.

# Protective finishes

Certain paint finishes need to be protected from exposure to water or steam, to the elements or simply from general wear and tear.

## Waxes

**Furniture waxes** come in an easily applicable form and in varying colours. If ready-coloured waxes are not available, they can be tinted with stainer or tinter, provided a suitable drying medium is added too. They are applied with a soft cloth and buffed up with 0000 grade steel wool. Old wax must be removed before starting work on a new surface, as it creates a barrier that will not take paint.

**Clear wax** protects with a soft sheen.

**Antiquing wax** is used to create a warm, antique look.

**Liming wax** imitates bleached wood by leaving a film of white in the grain and so works best on open-grained woods.

**Gilding wax** is used for highlighting mouldings and edges.

**Beeswax** is a traditional wax used to protect wood from drying out. It is available in liquid form (applied with a brush) and in paste form (applied with a lint-free cloth). The paste is a suitable alternative, although it is more difficult to use.

## Varnishes

**Oil-based varnish** is more robust than its water-based equivalent, but many types go yellow in sunlight or are naturally tinted. Always test a sample piece before use as they can change the coloration of a finish noticeably. Polyurethane is the most popular, but it is quite yellow and can be brittle.

**Resin-based water-soluble varnishes** do not yellow, are reasonably heat and water resistant, and are more user friendly. Available in matt and satin.

**Acrylic water-based varnishes** are quick-drying and available in matt, semi-gloss or gloss finishes.

**Spray varnishes** are non-yellowing and need to be treated with great care. They tend to offer only limited protection and work better on water-based effects. They are available in matt and gloss finishes.

**Shellac or knotting solution** provides a barrier between the wood knots and the painted finish, stopping the resin in the wood from bleeding through and discolouring the paint.

**French polish** is made from shellac, a natural resin, in liquid suspension. It is the classic finish for fine furniture, but correct application takes some skill to master.

**Button polish** is made from unbleached shellac buttons, and is darker and more cloudy than French polish. It is a great favourite with restorers to recreate 'old' finishes.

**Shellac sanding sealer** fills the grain in an open-grained wood such as mahogany and allows it to take a better finish.

protective finishes include: 1 spray varnish; 2 oil-based varnish; 3 shellac; 4 water-based varnish

gloss-finish varnish

satin-finish varnish

matt-finish varnish

softening brush

flogging brush

dragging brush

stippling brush

stencil brushes

gilder's mop brush

# Brushes, sponges and rollers

One of the secrets of success in decorative painting is to know and use the correct tool for the job. Will it produce a fine enough line? Will it produce the surface texture I want? Always buy the best tools you can afford. They pay for themselves in the end, especially if they are properly cared for.

Remember also that brushes are made of different materials, as are rollers and sponges. Nylon and synthetic brushes work well enough with water-based paints, while oil-based paints generally require better-quality hair or bristle brushes. These can be expensive, but are worth the outlay.

**Softening brushes** such as the high-quality badger-hair softener are very expensive. A hog-hair softener or dusting brush is cheaper and can also be used to remove dust.
**Flogging brushes** are used for wood graining and some marble effects. They can also be used for dragging.
**Dragging brushes** are long-bristled brushes that are used for the dragging and graining techniques. An alternative would be an ordinary basecoat brush, but the effect is less subtle.
**Stippling brushes** come in a variety of shapes and sizes that produce different textural effects. They can be made of bristle or rubber and this dictates price.
**Stencil brushes** can be domed or flat and are available in different sizes. Made from hard-wearing bristle they produce a fine stipple effect when used over a stencil.
**Gilder's mops** are soft brushes of camel or squirrel hair used primarily in gilding to remove surplus leaf or to apply metal powders. A soft artist's brush makes a good alternative.
**Fitch brushes** are usually made of hog hair and come in shapes such as round, oval, flat or chiselled. They are used for

fitch brushes        lining brushes        artist's brushes

mixing small quantities of paint, cutting in, and painting mouldings and small areas. They are also useful for spattering because of their stiff bristles. Use the tip of the brush to work the paint. Start with a flat 13 mm (½ in), a round 6–13 mm (¼–½ in), and possibly a chiselled 13 mm (½ in).

**Lining brushes** are essential for line and other decorative applications. They hold the paint in long bristles and allow easy flow. They are also ideal for marbling. Build up a collection starting with sizes 0, 1 and 3.

**Artist's brushes** come in a variety of shapes and sizes. They range in quality from the best and most expensive sable to the more affordable hog-hair and nylon. They are excellent for cutting in on panels and for working in tight corners. A fine artist's brush can be used instead of a lining brush.

**Varnishing brushes** come in a wide range of sizes. They are thickly bristled and can be flat or domed. Ideally purchase a 50 mm (2 in) flat brush.

**Household paintbrushes** come in a range of sizes. For priming and undercoating it is best to use a straight-edge brush, and for cutting in edges, a chisel-edge brush. Choose the size that is most suitable for the job and the largest you feel comfortable with. A good range would be 13 mm (½ in), 25 mm (1 in), 50 mm (2 in), 100 mm (4 in), and 125 mm (5 in).

**Tooth brushes or nail brushes** can be used to spatter colour.

**Wire brushes** are used for preparing and cleaning surfaces and for liming techniques.

**Sponges** are used for mottling, stippling and colorwashing. Use a natural sponge, the surface of which is pitted, or a synthetic sponge that has a smoother surface and is cheaper. A prepared cellulose decorator's sponge is ideal for colourwashing as it will not show marks.

**Rollers** can be used to apply base colours, plaster coats and textured effects. Radiator rollers can be used on inaccessible areas and small roller heads can be used for stenciling. Many types of roller heads are available including foam, textured and sheepskin. Avoid using foam rollers with oil-based paints as they be may affected by the white spirit in the paint.

household brushes

varnishing brush

tooth brush

wire brushes

decorator's and natural sponges

sheepskin roller          small sheepskin roller heads

small foam roller heads          small textured roller head

rubber combs

heart grainers

feathers

scraper

filler knives

bucket

hawk

float

lint-free cloth

plastic paint kettle

dust cover

# Other equipment

**Combs** are used for combing glazing liquid and textured paints. They are available in rubber, leather and steel, and come in various grades of teeth. For small jobs, you could make your own from thin plastic or stiff card.

**Heart grainers** are used for wood graining and some marble finishes. They are usually made of rubber and come in different widths and grades.

**Feathers** are used in marbling for very fine graining instead of fine artist's brushes or sword liners. You can buy goose or swan feathers, but any clean, sturdy feather can be used.

**Filler knives** are the best flexible metal blades to use for mixing, applying and smoothing plaster and stucco. The blades can also be useful for scraping out paint containers and cleaning up spillages.

**Scrapers** are an essential tool for stripping paint and varnish and for cleaning up flaking areas. They are also useful for filling cracks and holes when using ready-made fillers.

**A plasterer's hawk and float** is used for applying plaster.

**Paint containers** are necessary for pouring out paint into useable amounts and also for mixing paints and plasters. Paint kettles, roller trays and buckets are available in metal or plastic. An environmentally friendly and cost-effective approach is to recycle durable household waste items – for example, a large jar or plastic container for a paint kettle, and a shallow container for a paint tray, as long as they are deep and wide enough to hold and mix your material.

**Lint-free cloths** will not shed their fibres during use. They are ideal for wiping down and removing dust from surfaces. You will need them for ragging and other techniques, applying waxes and polishing. They can also be used to dampen in the relevant solvent, remove any mistakes, clean up spills, and wipe your brushes, paint containers and hands. You can use clean old clothes, but make sure they are made of absorbent natural fibers that will not shed during use.

**Dust covers** protect furniture and vulnerable surfaces from paint spills. Save old sheets and curtains to use as dust covers. Newspapers can be used as an alternative to sheeting, but newsprint can leave marks.

spirit level

plumb-bob or plumbline

tape measure

card,
carbon paper,
steel rule, ruler,
pencils, and eraser

stencil card

craft knife

scissors

wire or
steel wool

masking tape

wet-dry sandpaper
and block

**A spirit level** helps mark out accurate horizontal lines.

**A plumb-bob or plumbline** will give perfect vertical lines.

**A pencil, eraser and chalk** are used for marking out. Chalk is often preferable as it is easily removed and will not mark the surface. However, a pencil line will give greater accuracy.

**A ruler, steel rule and tape measure** will be needed for measuring and marking out. Use a steel rule for cutting against to make your craft knife less likely to slip.

**Graph, tracing and carbon paper** are all available in sheet or book form from stationer's or artist's supply shops.

**Card** can be obtained in varying thicknesses and can be prepared for use as a sample board and to texture paint.

**Stencil card** is also known as manila or oiled card. This is flexible and strong but will eventually become saturated with paint, and stencils will buckle or shrink. It is best to cut several copies of a design if it is to be used repeatedly. An alternative is transparent stencil acetate, or Mylar. Make sure you cut your stencil on a self-heal cutting mat.

**Sharp scissors, craft knife or scalpel** are essential for decoupage, cutting straight edges and stencils.

**Masking tape** come in a variety of sizes and levels of adhesive. Low-tack masking tape is better for use over new paintwork. Both can be used to mask out areas and position stencils.

**Wire or steel wool** comes in different grades and can be used for keying (preparing) most surfaces to take paint. Fine wire wool can be used to apply wax, to smooth a surface and to lightly lift off a top coat and reveal base colours.

**Sandpaper** comes in a selection of grades. Wet-dry sandpaper is more expensive, but lasts longer and is more controllable.

**Sanding blocks** are useful for preparing larger sufaces, but are not recommended for some of the more delicate finishing techniques as they are hard and can leave marks.

**Everyday household items** come in handy for miscellaneous uses. Use a screwdriver for opening paint cans, spoons for measuring paint and powders, a whisk for mixing paint and fine plaster, a sieve for sprinkling whiting, and a heatproof bowl for mixing size, gesso and bole.

# Basic techniques

Although individual paint effects are covered in detail on pages 40–251, there are a number of general techniques that you should master before you start. These include various ways of preparing a surface; methods of applying paint; finishing techniques that will keep your paint looking good; how to keep your brushes and other equipment in serviceable condition; and how to work safely.

## Surface preparation

Careful preparation is essential, as the quality of your base surface will affect the look of your final paintwork. Different surfaces require different treatments.

### Cleaning surfaces

The surface must first be thoroughly cleaned: quite apart from the fact that surface grime will dirty any new paint you apply, paint will not adhere to grease and dirt. Wash the surface with household detergent diluted in water and then wipe it down with a clean, damp cloth. For very dirty surfaces, use a solution of sugar soap and rinse off with clean water.

### Preparing plaster

Fill any cracks or holes with interior filler and sand smooth when dry. For large cracks, apply filler with a trowel; for small cracks and dents, use a filling knife. After sanding, wipe the surface with a clean, damp, lint-free cloth to remove all dust.

Wash down dirty surfaces with a solution of sugar soap.

### Preparing wood

Wood that has previously been painted or varnished must be sanded to remove loose material and leave a smooth working surface to which the paint will adhere. Choose coarse-, medium-, or fine-grade sandpaper, depending on the state of the existing surface and the level of smoothness you require. If you are preparing an uneven or previously treated surface such as wood panelling, you may need to use a wire brush to clean inside grooves or other areas that are difficult to sand. Always sand wood following the direction of the grain. Always wear a face mask to avoid inhaling dust.

For layers of thick, uneven paint and varnish that cannot be

Prepare wood with a wire brush and sandpaper.

rubbed back by sandpaper alone, use a commercial paint stripper. Wear protective gloves and a face mask and follow the manufacturer's instructions carefully. Apply the paint stripper liberally and leave it to soak in for at least 30 minutes before removing the paint with a metal paint scraper.

Water-based paints will not adhere to surfaces that have previously been treated with oil-based stains, or waxed or polished. To remove oil-based stains, dip medium-grade steel wool in white spirit and scrub the surface with a circular motion, wearing protective gloves. Waxes, polishes and shellacs can be removed in the same way using medium-grade steel wool and methylated spirits. Wipe down with diluted detergent. When dry, sand thoroughly.

Fill any sections of missing grain or cracks with commercial wood filler. Allow the filler to dry, then sand. Do not use resin-based fillers if you are using an acrylic primer. With paint finishes that require a very smooth surface, very open-grain wood will need to be filled. Use fine commercial filler designed for walls for this purpose. Seal knots on new, bare wood by applying knot sealer with a paintbrush to prevent resin from seeping through to the final paint finish.

Apply paint stripper with a brush and leave to soak.

Remove the paint and paint stripper with a scraper.

Remove oil-based stains, wax, or polish with medium-grade steel wool.

## Priming your surface

Primers seal the surface, provide initial coverage and create a bond between the surface and the paint.

### Priming plaster

Fresh or previously untreated plaster, or very porous surfaces, should be sealed with PVA or white glue, or white emulsion paint diluted with water before you apply the paint; otherwise you will not have sufficient time to work before the paint dries, as the surface will absorb the moisture in the paint. Brush the sealer or diluted paint on evenly and leave it to dry completely before you apply the paint effect.

### Priming wood

For wood, the type of primer depends on both the surface and on the type of paint you are planning to use. In most instances, commercial acrylic primer is suitable, but the instructions in the projects will tell you exactly what to use.

Use diluted PVA or white glue, or white emulsion paint to seal plaster.

Mask around light switches.

Mix paints and glazes in a paint kettle.

Load your brush to a maximum of two-thirds of the bristle length.

Use tape to mask colour edges and remove it once the paint is dry.

# Getting ready to paint

Carefully mask all fixtures and fittings, light switches, electrical sockets and the skirting board with masking tape, making sure the tape is pressed down firmly.

Arrange all the paints and equipment you need in the centre of the room and try to keep them as neat and tidy as possible while you work.

## Mixing paints

Always mix paints and glazes in a paint kettle. Make up more than you think you will need, because it is virtually impossible to achieve the same consistency and colour twice, especially if you're working in a hurry. Try out colour combinations on a piece of spare board and position it in different parts of the room at different times of the day to get a good idea of its effect under all circumstances and lights.

# Using a brush

Brushes can be used in a variety of ways, but whatever effect you are creating remember these general guidelines. Always use a clean, dry brush. Never load your brush any further than three-quarters of the way up the bristles. Be sure to clean your brushes thoroughly after use to prolong their life.

## Painting straight edges

To paint completely straight bands of colour (for example, when painting a pattern), mark out the edges of the relevant area with masking tape. Stick the tape in position, with one edge on the line where the first colour will finish, and then paint up to that line and onto the tape. When the paint is dry, just peel off the tape to leave a perfectly straight edge.

To get a second colour to line up perfectly with the first, wait until the first colour is completely dry and then stick tape along the edge you have just painted.

Always make sure the tape is pressed down firmly, or else the paint may creep under the edge. Remove the tape as soon as possible after painting – the longer it is left on the surface, the more chance there is of a sticky residue being left behind:

## Dry-brushing

In dry-brushing, undiluted paint is applied in random directions, leaving a little base colour exposed in places. The effect can be used to create or exaggerate the texture on a surface or to suggest the effect of paint fading over time.

As the name suggests, the brush is used almost dry. Dip the end of the bristles into paint and scrape off the excess on the edge of the paint kettle. Hold the brush almost parallel to the surface and apply the paint using just the tip. Turn the brush over to use the paint on the other side of the bristles and change the angle of the strokes for a random effect.

dry-brushing

## Stippling

Stippling is a delicate and simple technique to add colour and subtle texture to a surface. As the application is so fine, blending of colours can be achieved with ease. Stippling can be used to create a uniform and smooth background for mural or lining work and was traditionally used with dragging and oil glazes on furniture and interiors.

Work in a dust-free environment to minimise the transfer of dust particles that the bristles of the stippling brush might pick up. Dip the stippling brush lightly into the paint and dab off any excess on paper or cloth. Stipple by dabbing the bristle ends onto the surface.

stippling

## Dragging

Dragging is a simple method of creating a fine, linear texture with a brush and can be used for a variety of paint effects.

Dip just the tip of the brush into the paint or glaze. Hold the brush in one hand and place your other hand near the tip of the bristles – this will help you control the brush. Pull the brush down through the wet paint, trying to keep the line as straight as possible. For the next section of paint, overlap the previous strip slightly and drag as before.

dragging

## Flogging

Flogging is used to create some wood-graining and marble effects. Starting at the bottom of the glazed or painted area, hit the surface in a flogging action with the flat tip of the brush, working upwards if you are painting a vertical surface such as a wall or away from you if you are working flat.

flogging

lining

softening

## Lining

Some designs require the creation of fine lines – for example, to create the effect of tiles or flagstones. Coachliners are the traditional tools used by signwriters, but they can be difficult to control. A good alternative is a lining brush. The trick is to paint smoothly and confidently: if you hesitate, the line will wobble. Use an even pressure all the way. When working on a dry surface, place the little finger of your painting hand on the work surface to help steady your touch.

## Softening

Softening is a technique that is frequently used with paint effects to soften and blur hard brush strokes or to blend one colour into another. The brush is generally used dry. Hold the brush handle near the base of the bristles and use long, sweeping crisscrossing movements. To soften hard brush strokes, use the softener in the opposite direction to the original strokes. To blend colours one into another, use the softener in the same direction as the original brush strokes.

### CARING FOR BRUSHES

- Before using a new brush for the first time, rinse it in clean water to get rid of any loose bristles that would otherwise stick to the painted surface.
- Clean all brushes immediately after use.
- To clean a brush used for oil-based paint, rinse it out well in a paint kettle or bowl using white spirit until as much of the colour as possible has been removed. Then wash it in warm water with lots of dishwashing liquid until all the paint and white spirit have washed away.
- To clean a brush used for water-based paint, wash it in warm water and dishwashing liquid. If the paint has dried on areas of the bristles, use a small nailbrush to remove it.
- After washing brushes, smooth out the bristles and stand the brushes upright in a container to dry. Always store brushes carefully to avoid the bristles being bent.

Before using a new brush rinse in clean water and check for loose bristles when dry.

# Using a roller

Always use a roller with a tray. Pour some paint into the paint well, taking care not to overfill it: a depth of about 2 cm (¾ in) is usually sufficient.

## Loading a roller

Load your roller by rolling it lightly into the paint and then rolling it back and forth on the dimpled surface of the paint tray to cover the roller evenly. Do not overload or you will get drips. Roll your surface, first in one direction and then at right angles to get an even coverage.

loading a roller

A roller will not paint right up to internal angles; stop painting about 2.5 cm (1 in) from the angle and complete the job using a paintbrush. Stipple the edges and corners rather than finishing with a brush stroke or the textural difference will cause the paint effect to appear to have lines and darker edges. Rollers can be used with an extension pole to paint a ceiling or upper section of a wall without the use of ladders.

## Cleaning a roller

Remove the sleeve from the roller and clean it in the appropriate solvent for the paint used. Squeeze out as much excess water as you can and leave to dry thoroughly before storing in a box or bag to keep them clean.

Roll your surface in one direction and then again at right angles.

For oil-based paint, rinse the brush out well using white spirit until as much of the colour as possible has been removed.

After washing, wipe off excess liquid on a clean cloth and smooth out the bristles before standing the brushes upright in a container to dry.

## To Prepare a Sponge

Rinse the sponge in water and detergent to remove any yellow dye. When it is dry, cut the sponge in half with a sharp knife.

Trim around the heat-sealed edges and tear off the outer sides.

Pick off pieces around the edges and corners. This gives an irregular shape similar to a natural sponge, that is more suitable for decorating.

colourwashing in a figure-of-eight

# Using a sponge

Many paint effects require the paint to be applied with a sponge, rather than a brush or a roller. For preference, use a cellulose decorator's sponge, which is close in texture to natural sponge but considerably less expensive. To prepare your sponge for use see left.

## Colourwashing

Do not dip the sponge in the paint, as it can easily become overloaded. Instead, brush paint onto the surface of the sponge. Apply the paint to the surface in a figure-of-eight movement, as this makes any marks less visible. Try to work in an area approximately 60 cm (2 ft) square, keeping the edges of each application irregular. If you are working with a strong colour it is more difficult to control the washes, so try to thin down the application of paint around the edge of each application, where the washes meet, by flipping the sponge over to the clean, paint-free side and lifting off some of the colour around the edges. Building up thin layers of dilute paint gives a smoother, more uniform finish and a deeper colour. Don't rush by applying thicker paint in fewer layers. Always work with a damp sponge and rinse it out regularly with detergent and water.

## Stippling

You can create a textured finish by stippling paint on with a cellulose sponge. To achieve a fine covering when using a fine stencil, use a foam sponge with a dense surface or a foam roller head. Dab the paint on with a 'pouncing' motion.

## Cleaning your sponge

Clean the sponge in the appropriate solvent for the paint used. Squeeze out as much excess water as you can and leave to dry thoroughly before storing.

# Protective finishes

Having put so much time and effort into creating your paint effect, you will want to protect it and make sure it lasts as long as possible. The instructions in the projects will tell you what finish is most appropriate for each effect.

### Applying liquid varnishes

Load the brush and work over a limited area at a time. Brush out each stroke with a cross-hatching motion to prevent the brush strokes from being visible. Keep working until the surface has begun to dry slightly, as this will prevent any drips. Always view the surface from different angles to see if you can spot any patches that have been missed. You may need to sand and remove dust between coats for a deeper, smoother finish, or to apply more than one layer for a better overall coverage.

### Applying beeswax

Beeswax should be applied to the surface with a soft, lint-free cloth. Wait for a few minutes for the wax to penetrate the surface, then remove any excess and buff with a clean cloth.

### Applying shellac

Shellac is used to seal gilded and decoupaged effects, and on paint, for a lacquer-style finish before varnishing. The solvent in shellac evaporates very quickly, so careful application is required. Dip a varnish brush into the shellac and glide it onto the surface. After laying on, brush through only twice before evaporation starts, or the smooth look will be spoiled. Wait two hours before applying a top coat of varnish.

# Storing paints and varnishes

Store any half-empty paint tins upside down: any air that has entered the container will go to the bottom of the tin. When you turn it over to use it again, the paint at the top should still be fluid and useable. Keep any mixes or glazes in sealed and labelled containers rather than throwing them away or returning them to the tin.

applying liquid varnish

applying wax

buffing with a lint-free cloth

applying shellac

# Health and safety

- Always wear a dust mask and protective gloves when working with oil- and alcohol-based products, plasters, powders and varnishes and waxes.
- If you have sensitive skin, wear gloves even for water-based products, as lengthy exposure can cause your skin to dry out. Thin surgical gloves are ideal, as they provide protection without impeding your movements.
- When sanding or using toxic products, wear a dust mask and goggles to protect your eyes and lungs.
- Always work in a well ventilated area.
- When working up a ladder be sure that the feet are solidly positioned, will not slip, and the braces are securely locked down. Never try to extend beyond comfortable reach as the ladder could tip over.
- Remember to protect all other surfaces with dust covers to prevent possible damage.
- Do not throw rags soaked with volatile liquid substances such as white spirit directly into the dustbin, but lay them out flat to dry before you discard them to prevent the risk of them combusting.
- Label all containers clearly, and keep all chemicals and paints out of the reach of young children – preferably under lock and key.
- Try to avoid using containers which could easily be mistaken for another product by their shape or colour. Even if they are properly labeled.
- Whatever product you are using, always read and follow the manufacturer's instructions.

goggles

dust mask

Use extra strong gloves when working with more toxic products such as paint stripper.

ladder safety

# Paint effects
# selector

## 100 paint effects swatches for swift reference

Use this reference guide to choose the paint effect that is best for you and your home. With this comprehensive swatch selector, you can compare different styles and easily gauge which decorative effect is the most appealing. Paint effects have never been easier.

# Working with colour

**44–45** Two-tone colourwashing

**46–47** Mixed colourwashing

**48–49** Fake clouds

**50–51** Colourwashing a textured surface

**52–53** Colourwash and stipple mix

**54–55** Dry-brushing

**56–57** Make your own paint

**58–59** Stippling fade

**60–61** Linen effect

**62–63** Lacquer effect

**64–65** Transparent stripes

**66–67** Mondrian style

**68–69** Opaque stripes

**70–71** Roller patterning

**72–73** Roller spots

**74–75** Ragging

**76–77** Overlaying colours

**78–79** Spray paint and fabric patterning

**80–81** Lace stencil

**82–83** Scrim frottage

# Textured effects

**86–87** Sandstone

**88–89** Slate

**90–91** Terracotta

**92–93** Stone blockwork

**94–95** Limestone paving

**96–97** Imitation leather

**98–99** Imitation snakeskin

**100–101** Denim effect

**102–103** Imitation moiré silk

**104–105** Imitation suede panelling

**106–107** Stucco

**108–109** Rustic clay

**110–111** Aged plaster effect

**112–113** Gesso

**114–115** Combing

**116–117** Stencilling with filler and mica

**118–119** Crackle effect

**120–121** Craquelure

**122–123** Collage

**124–125** Collage and decoupage

# Traditional effects

 128–129 Sienna marble

 130–131 Breccia marble

 132–133 Carrara marble

 134–135 Rhodocrosite

 136–137 Granite

 138–139 Oak

 140–141 Pine

 142–143 Bird's-eye maple

 144–145 Fruitwood

 146–147 Mahogany

 148–149 Peeling paint

 150–151 Antiquing with coloured waxes

 152–153 Trompe l'oeil

 154–155 Drag and stipple with lining

 156–157 Fake parquet floor

 158–159 Porphyry

 160–161 Tortoiseshell

 162–163 Lapis lazuli

 164–165 Malachite

 166–167 Floating marble

# Metallic effects

**170–171** Metallic paints

**172–173** Metallic and matt paints

**174–175** Gold-painted squares

**176–177** Steel

**178–179** Rusted iron

**180–181** Verdigris

**182–183** Opalescent solid colour

**184–185** Opalescent and iridescent washes

**186–187** Mixing lustre paints

**188–189** Bronze powders

**190–191** Water gilding with real gold

**192–193** Oil gilding with real silver

**194–195** Imitation gold and silver transfer leaf

**196–197** Copper loose leaf

**198–199** Gilding on glass

**200–201** Metallic paint and metal leaf

**202–203** Oil and water on metal leaf

**204–205** Metallic paint patination

**206–207** Distressing with spirit dyes

**208–209** Chemical patination

# Patterns and motifs

**212–213** Irregular
patterning

**214–215** Regular
patterning

**216–217** Building up
colours

**218–219** Making a
large repeat stencil

**220–221** Simple mural

**222–223** Printing
blocks

**224–225** Vegetable
stamps

**226–227** Found-
material printing

**228–229** Frottage

**230–231** Sprayed
leaves and cut-outs

**232–233** Lining-paper
bands

**234–235** Circles

**236–237** Craquelure
stripes

**238–239** Outline
squares

**240–241** Wallpaper

**242–243** Wallpaper
border

**244–245** Acrylic spatter
and oil spray

**246–247** Simple
freehand painting

**248–249** Grisaille

**250–251** Decoupage
grisaille

# The paint effects

### 100 paint effects shown in step-by-step photographs

Use this accessible directory to find the paint effect or faux finish that's right for your space, and give a wall, a floor or indeed any surface a facelift. With clear instructions, comprehensive lists of readily obtainable materials and step-by-step techniques sequences, decorating your home has never been this easy!

above: collage bedhead with linen-effect walls and shelving units

# Working
## with colour

When using paints to decorative effect, the depth and intensity of colour that can be achieved is often bewildering to someone used to using flat paint, ready-mixed from a can. Therefore, a look at the possible application methods, using brushes, sponges, rollers and cloths, can enlighten the novice decorator. This chapter demonstrates the use of much of the equipment available and, more importantly, demonstrates the potential of the colour itself when limited tools are used.

To achieve the most interesting layers and washes, a humble sponge will suffice. A household paintbrush can be used with great dexterity to blend translucent glazes and solid paints. It is often a good idea to work within a limited range of colours initially, then expand as you become familiar with the characteristics of certain colours and how they combine. Successful balancing of warm and cold colours is an important step to master,  especially if you are trying to suggest space in a small area or create a relaxing atmosphere in a busy room.

The effects demonstrated are suitable for all surfaces, not just walls, so don't be afraid to use paint effects on furniture, floors, floorcloths or even exterior walls. At this stage the importance of preparation can not be emphasised enough. If you take the time to fully prepare your surface, the resulting paint finish will last that much longer.

# Two-tone colourwashing

## Materials and Equipment

Lime green matt emulsion
   paint for the base coat
Bright green acrylic paint
Matt acrylic glaze
Paint kettles
Roller and tray
Decorator's sponge
Household paintbrushes

Colourwashing is a simple technique that can be used to great effect. Building up layers of dilute paint produces depth and textural interest, even when using just one or two colours of a similar tone or hue. Clear glaze should be used to protect the effect when you have reached the required depth of colour. It is easy to repair a colourwash so remember to keep some of your mixes in airtight containers for future use.

1 *Apply the base coat with a roller. Dilute 1 part bright green acrylic paint with 3 parts water. Dampen a decorator's sponge and use a brush to load it with dilute paint. Wash colour over the surface using a figure-of-eight movement. Allow to dry.*

2 *Repeat Step 1 to apply a second colourwash layer in the same colour, to enhance the effect. Make sure you work systematically, covering the whole area evenly. Leave to dry.*

3 *Dilute 1 part lime green matt emulsion paint with 3 parts water and add a small amount of matt acrylic glaze to help fix the paint. Wash this over the deeper colour in a smooth, even layer. Leave to dry.*

4 *Add patches of the first deeper green glaze to increase the depth and texture in some areas. Allow to dry.*

5 *Repeat any of the steps as necessary, working with the deeper or the lighter green, to achieve the desired effect. The paint effect becomes more solid as you add more layers. Leave to dry.*

6 *Use a brush to apply clear glaze with regular brushstrokes. This will protect the finish from staining and damage. Work the glaze in a small area at a time to ensure an even coverage.*

# Mixed colourwashing

## Materials and Equipment

Pale lilac matt emulsion paint
  for the base coat
Acrylic paints: pink, warm blue
White matt emulsion paint
Roller and tray
Household paintbrushes
Decorator's sponge
Paint kettles
Matt acrylic glaze

This colourwash combines warm and cold colours to create a restful shade that will bring a harmonious, relaxing ambience to any room. The layers of pink and warm blue are softened with the pale lilac base colour to achieve a chalky finish. This effect demonstrates a different application of a colourwash to that shown on pages 44–45, since here the layers are built up with a strong pattern of cross-hatching.

1 Apply the base coat with a roller. Dilute 1 part pink acrylic paint with 2 parts water. Dampen a decorator's sponge and use a brush to load it with the dilute paint. Wash the colour on in a loose cross-hatching motion. Leave to dry.

2 Dilute warm blue acrylic paint as in Step 1, but add a touch of white matt emulsion paint to soften the colour. Use the sponge to apply the paint with the same cross-hatch movement. The colour will settle over the pink and suggest a purple. Leave to dry.

3 Add additional layers of blue colourwash to deepen the effect. Always keep the sponge moist and make sure it is cleaned well between applications to ensure the colours do not mix and muddy. Leave to dry.

4 Add some white to the pink and blue dilute paints and add more colourwashes to achieve the desired effect. Allow to dry.

5 Dilute 1 part pale lilac matt emulsion paint with 3 parts water and lightly and evenly wash this mix over the surface. The paint should be very watery so as not to obscure the previous layers.

6 Use a brush to apply matt acrylic glaze. This will make the wash colours shine through the top coat and protect the finish. Work the glaze in a small area at a time to ensure an even coverage.

# Fake clouds

## Materials and Equipment

Sky blue matt emulsion paint
   for the base coat
White matt emulsion paint
Acrylic paints: aqua blue, grey
Roller and tray
Decorator's sponge
Household paintbrush
Paint kettles
Matt acrylic glaze

Here is a simple way to suggest clouds using a sponge technique. The colour and shapes are applied lightly with areas of solidity and definition achieved through the build-up of layers. Initially the movement of the sponge is kept light and the edges of the cloud shapes soft, but you can rework the decoration to make it darker or more atmospheric. Additional detail is added using a little grey and more white to give extra depth.

1 *Apply the base coat with a roller. Mix equal amounts of white matt emulsion paint and water. Dampen a decorator's sponge and use a brush to load it with the dilute paint. Use the sponge to loosely apply cloud shapes to the surface. Leave to dry. Add more white to the edges of the clouds to suggest solidity.*

2 *Use a damp sponge to add a touch of aqua blue acrylic paint here and there to vary the tone. Apply the paint lightly so the white is still visible underneath.*

3 *Add more white as necessary, to suggest thicker clouds in places. Building up the cloud shapes with multiple layers adds depth and makes them appear more realistic.*

4 *Use white matt emulsion paint on the side of a damp sponge to add highlights where the sun shines onto the clouds. Use grey acrylic paint on a clean damp sponge to add lowlights where the clouds are in shadow.*

5 *Repeat any of the steps to build up layers and create atmosphere. Keep the washes light so as not to obscure previous work.*

6 *Highlight the edges of the clouds once more, using white matt emulsion paint on a damp sponge. Protect by applying matt acrylic glaze.*

# Colourwashing a textured surface

## Materials and Equipment

PVA or white glue
Pale cream matt emulsion
   paint for the base coat
Acrylic paints: burnt sienna,
   burnt umber
Roller and tray
Decorator's sponge
Household paintbrushes
Paint kettles
Fine-grade wet-dry sandpaper
Matt acrylic glaze

When you strip a wall, you don't always find a perfect plaster surface underneath. Working a paint effect over chipped and damaged plaster may appear a daunting challenge, but colourwashing a textured surface can emphasise the beauty of the imperfections and add depth to the wall. Here, dilute washes of earth colours are built up to give a soft clay colour, similar to that of a worn plaster wall.

1 Seal the wall with PVA or white glue and apply the base coat with a roller. Dilute 1 part burnt sienna acrylic paint with 3 parts water. Dampen a decorator's sponge and use a brush to load it with the dilute paint. Wash over the surface in a figure-of-eight motion, pushing the colour well into recesses.

2 While the paint is still wet, turn the sponge over and wipe it over the paint. This should lift some colour from the surface but leave it still deep in the recesses. Re-dampen the sponge and follow Steps 1–2 in the same area again, if necessary. Let dry.

3 Dilute burnt umber acrylic paint as in Step 1 and wash it on as before. Lift off the surface colour with a damp sponge. You may have to rub quite hard if the colour has settled too much. Try to leave the paint in the recesses.

4 The two colours will have given the textured surface an appearance of depth and age. This can be emphasised by lightly sanding the top surface with fine-grade wet-dry sandpaper.

5 If you want to add patches of colour again do so now. Due to the sanding the paint will sit on the smoother surface and will require more effort when rubbing into the recesses.

6 Protect the finished effect by applying several coats of matt acrylic glaze with a household paintbrush. Work the glaze in a small area at a time to ensure an even coverage.

# Colourwash and stipple mix

## Materials and Equipment

Pale cream matt emulsion
   paint for the base coat
Acrylic paints: burnt sienna,
   yellow ochre, ultramarine
White matt emulsion paint
Roller and tray
Decorator's sponge
Household paintbrushes
Paint kettles
Matt acrylic glaze

Colourful washes and stippled patches can imitate the transparent glow given by a stained-glass window. To achieve the best result vary the intensity of the washes by carefully building up the colours. A mix of warm colours is balanced by the introduction of areas of blue, like dappled light. If the colours become too dark you can lighten the effect by washing over the surface with the base colour and repeating the technique.

1 *Apply the base coat with a roller. Dilute 1 part burnt sienna acrylic paint with 3 parts water. Dampen a decorator's sponge and use a brush to load it with dilute paint. Wash the colour on with a figure-of-eight movement, working the paint until dry.*

2 *Dilute yellow ochre acrylic paint as in Step 1 and apply to a clean sponge. Use the sponge to lightly stipple – dabbing rather than wiping – the colour on in patches. Leave to dry. Rinse out the sponge well before applying the next colour.*

3 *Dilute ultramarine acrylic paint as before, adding a little white matt emulsion paint to soften the colour. Repeat the stipple technique but do not apply too much blue because it will contrast significantly against the warmer colours. It should appear as no more than a slight bruising. Leave to dry.*

4 *Apply some of the pale cream matt emulsion paint to a very damp sponge, then wash on a thin layer, going back to the figure-of-eight movement. This will add depth and soften the contrasting colours. Let dry.*

5 *Continue, repeating the steps, until you achieve the desired colour. Patches of additional layers will give a varying strength of colour. Do not over-work the layers or the colours will lose luminosity.*

6 *Glazing the finished effect with matt acrylic glaze protects it and makes the colours show up more. Use a household paintbrush and work in a small area at a time to ensure an even coverage.*

# Dry-brushing

## Materials and Equipment

Acrylic primer
Pale cream matt emulsion
  paint for the base coat
Matt emulsion paints: orange,
  mid-yellow, light yellow
Matt acrylic glaze
Paint kettles
Household paintbrushes
Decorator's sponge
Medium- and fine-grade
  wet-dry sandpaper

The dry-brushing technique involves loading just the bristles of the brush with paint before applying it loosely so it does not obscure the previous layer. This effect is often used to suggest texture on a bland surface or to exaggerate the texture of an uneven surface. If worked over wood, as here, the brush should be directed against the grain in short strokes. Here, the effect suggests that the sun has faded the paint.

1 Prime the surface with one coat of acrylic primer and apply the base coat with a paintbrush. Add a little matt acrylic glaze to orange matt emulsion paint and brush the mix into the recesses between the boards.

2 Load a small amount of mid-yellow matt emulsion paint onto the end of a brush and use loose, random brushstrokes to apply the paint. Do not cover the surface with a solid coat but let previous paint coats remain visible in places. Leave to dry.

3 Follow Step 2 to dry-brush a layer of light yellow matt emulsion paint using repeated short strokes in various directions. This layer will sit on top of the stronger colours, giving the appearance of a lighter, sun-bleached paint.

4 To add to the texture, lightly dry-brush on some pale cream matt emulsion paint. This will enhance the aged effect of the lighter yellow. Try to brush this in a random way and be careful not to obscure the previous colour too much. Let dry.

5 Check the effect when the paint is dry and repeat any of the steps to build up the finish. When you are satisfied, leave the paint overnight to dry.

6 Use medium-grade wet-dry sandpaper to lightly rub down the finish, sanding off the top layer in places and bringing out the base colours. Wipe over the surface with a damp sponge. Repeat the sanding with a fine-grade paper to give a smooth finish.

# Make your own paint

## Materials and Equipment

Pale blue matt emulsion paint
  for the base coat
Casein or milk-based paints
  (see page 17): light blue,
  mid-blue, dark blue
Paint kettles
Household paintbrushes
Fine-grade wet-dry sandpaper
Matt acrylic glaze

Casein – a form of traditional, milk-based paint – was widely used before the introduction of matt emulsion paint and gives a smooth matt finish with a chalky consistency. If casein is not available, a prepared or mixable milk paint is suitable. Brushstrokes will remain visible, so use this paint in an area where a textured surface is appropriate.

1 *Apply the base coat with a paintbrush. Make sure the surface is free from dust and grease. Use a brush to apply a coat of light blue casein paint in an even layer, cross-hatching to limit the visible brushstrokes. When first applied the colour appears transparent. Allow to dry to an opaque finish.*

2 *Use the same cross-hatching technique to apply a layer of the darkest blue casein paint. Let dry.*

3 *Load the tip of a clean brush with mid-blue casein paint and use a dry-brushing technique (see pages 54–55) to apply the mix. Use short strokes to blend in the light and dark paints. Leave to dry.*

4 *Dry-brush lightly over with the first, palest blue to give a chalky effect. Leave to dry.*

5 *If the texture has built up too much, lightly sand the surface with fine-grade wet-dry sandpaper. Repeat any of the steps to achieve the desired intensity of colour and leave to dry.*

6 *Lightly sand the surface once more before sealing with matt acrylic glaze, applied with a brush. Work the glaze in a small area at a time to ensure an even coverage.*

# Stippling fade

## Materials and Equipment

Pale cream matt emulsion
 paint for the base coat
Matt emulsion paints: dark
 green, light green, white
Matt acrylic glaze
Roller and tray
Paint kettles
Stippling brush, hog-hair
 softening brush, household
 paintbrush

Stippling creates a wonderfully uniform and smooth finish and is an easy way to blend colours. The fine blending made possible by this technique lends itself to obtaining some wonderful fades of dark to light colours. It is important to have a dust-free environment to work in as the bristles of the stippling brush can pick up and transfer particles that are difficult to remove.

1 Apply the base coat with a roller. Mix 2 parts dark green matt emulsion paint to 1 part matt acrylic glaze. Dip the bristles of a stippling brush into the glaze and dab off the excess. Stipple the glaze on by dabbing the flat of the bristles against the surface. Cover with a light coat and let dry.

2 Mix light green matt emulsion paint and matt acrylic glaze as in Step 1 and stipple all over as before. An even coverage is important so work over small areas at a time and keep the glaze evenly picked up on the brush.

3 Begin to suggest a fading of dark into light green by increasing the stippling density of the darker green colour in one area. Here we are working from dark at the top to light below.

4 Emphasise the fade by increasing the difference in shading, adding more of the lighter green to its designated area. The lighter green can be stippled almost solid.

5 Carefully blend the meeting point of the two greens with a light stippling of both colours. Use a hog-hair softening brush when working on the blending areas for a finer result.

6 You can enhance this shading by adding some white paint to the lightest colour mix and by increasing the density of the stippling. Protect the finish by applying matt acrylic glaze.

# Linen effect

## Materials and Equipment

Pale cream matt emulsion
paint for the base coat
Matt emulsion paints: taupe,
hessian
Matt acrylic glaze
Roller and tray
Paint kettles
Household paintbrushes

The light texture of this paint effect is built up to suggest an expensive linen fabric covering. If you are experienced with a dragging brush it is possible to achieve a longer, more uniform series of horizontal and vertical lines to suggest a looser weave of linen. When using a different colour combination remember to keep the tones similar and start with a sample area to check the strength of colour required.

1 *Apply the base coat with a roller. Mix equal amounts of taupe matt emulsion paint and matt acrylic glaze and add a splash of water. Dip just the tip of a paintbrush into the mix. Apply the glaze by dragging the brush vertically from top to bottom to produce a series of short lines. Try to keep the lines as straight as possible. Leave to dry.*

2 *Mix a hessian-coloured glaze as before and repeat the same dragging technique, this time working horizontally, across the vertical lines. Short brushstrokes will ensure the lines are as straight as possible.*

3 *Add occasional darker dragged lines of the first glaze mix. Keep the lines broken to suggest the uneven weave of linen fabric.*

4 *Mix equal amounts of pale cream matt emulsion paint and matt acrylic glaze and add broken lines to areas that have become too solid. Leave to dry.*

5 *Repeat any of the previous steps to achieve an even texture and regular pattern.*

6 *Dilute 1 part matt acrylic glaze with 2 parts water, then mix 1 part pale cream matt emulsion paint with 3 parts dilute glaze. Apply this with a household paintbrush to protect the finish and add a soft top coat to unify the overall look.*

# Lacquer effect

## Materials and Equipment

Pale pink acrylic eggshell for
the base coat
Red acrylic gloss paint
Household paintbrushes,
hog-hair softening brush
Medium- and fine-grade
wet-dry sandpaper
Clear (liquid) beeswax or
high-gloss varnish
Lint-free cloths

This is a simulation of the high-gloss lacquer finish traditionally used in Japan and China. The paint used is actually a water-based gloss, which means the layers will dry quickly and can be sanded and repainted many times in one day. The build-up of layers gives a longer-lasting finish than a single, solid coat, and achieves a translucency and depth that cannot be matched by flat colour.

1 Apply the base coat with a paintbrush. When the eggshell paint is completely dry, sand the surface with medium- then fine-grade wet-dry sandpaper. Use a circular motion and regularly change the paper.

2 Use a paintbrush to apply the first layer of red acrylic gloss in broad, loose strokes. Repeat the strokes over the surface until a smooth glaze of red covers the pink. Leave to dry.

3 Repeat the circular sanding motion with fine-grade wet-dry sandpaper. Clean off any dust.

4 Brush on another layer of red gloss as before. Cross the brushstrokes randomly and regularly until smooth. Leave to dry.

5 Sand and reglaze the red, following Steps 3–4, as often as necessary to reach the required density. Soften the final coat by brushing over in a variety of directions with a hog-hair softening brush while it is semi-wet. Let dry and finish with a light sanding.

6 Apply a coat of beeswax with a lint-free cloth (you will find liquid beeswax easier to apply than the paste form) or a coat of high-gloss varnish with a brush. Use a clean, dry cloth to buff it to a smooth sheen.

# Transparent stripes

## Materials and Equipment

Pale cream matt emulsion
  paint for the base coat
Tape measure, pencil,
  chalk line
Matt emulsion paints: warm
  blue, pink
Matt acrylic glaze
Paint kettles
Rollers and trays
Household paintbrush
Medium-grade
  wet-dry sandpaper
Damp sponge

Stripes make a bold statement, but using transparent glaze allows the introduction of a strong pattern while keeping the colours low key. Sanding the glaze when dry also softens the edges of each stripe. Vary the width of the stripes to fit the dimensions of the room: to give visual impact to a large wall, use plenty of stripes of varying widths; but use fewer, wider bands for an area that is busy with details.

1 Apply the base coat with a roller. Use a tape measure and pencil to mark the wall with a pattern of stripes of varying widths. Use a chalk line to give the first vertical to measure from. Remember that the cream base coat will form some of the stripes.

2 Dilute 1 part warm blue matt emulsion paint with 2 parts matt acrylic glaze. Pour the mix into a roller tray and thinly load the roller. Roll on the glaze, following the first chalk line, to paint a broad blue stripe. Paint in the other blue stripes and leave to dry. Wash off the chalk line with a damp sponge.

3 Follow Step 2 to roll on pink stripes between the blue stripes, leaving stripes of the cream base coat on either side. The edges can be uneven.

4 Working carefully by eye, roll a stripe of pink down the centre of alternate broad blue stripes. Leave to dry.

5 Touch up areas of cream paint as necessary, using a brush to stipple between the bands of colour. Allow to dry.

6 Sand the stripes with medium-grade wet-dry sandpaper, using a regular movement. This will allow some of the cream to break through the glaze, make the finish more chalky and soften the uneven rollered edges.

# Mondrian style

### Materials and Equipment

Acrylic primer
White matt emulsion paint for
the base coat
Tape measure, pencil, masking
tape, craft knife
Matt emulsion paints: red,
blue, yellow, black
Rollers and trays
Household paintbrush
Matt acrylic varnish

This graphic, geometric pattern can be applied to any surface, from a whole wall to a single item of furniture. The colours must be carefully planned, so it is a good idea to draw up a coloured paper plan of the design layout before marking up the decoration. Adding the paint in rollered layers means that it will hold firmly and last well.

1 Roll on a coat of acrylic primer and apply the base coat with a paintbrush. Use a tape measure, masking tape and a craft knife to mark out a series of squares and rectangles. Refer to a Mondrian print for help. The masking tape should cover what will later become the thin black lines.

2 Roll on red matt emulsion paint as evenly as possible. Leave to dry and roll on a second layer to achieve a solid colour. You may find it useful to lightly mark the squares with pencil to indicate which colours are to be used where.

3 Roll on blue matt emulsion paint in the appropriate places as before. Repeat with yellow matt emulsion paint. Leave to dry.

4 Make pencil marks along the edges of the masking tape on both sides and remove the tape.

5 Remask, aligning the tape with the pencil lines to mark the black bands. The edges should be as straight as possible.

6 Paint in the black lines with a roller. Leave to dry and apply a second coat if necessary. Once dry, carefully remove the masking tape and apply matt acrylic varnish with a household paintbrush.

# Opaque stripes

### Materials and Equipment

Pale cream matt emulsion
paint for the base coat
Chalk line, masking tape,
cotton fabric, plumbline
Matt emulsion paints: pink,
yellow, lilac, bright green
Rollers and trays
Household paintbrush
Fine-grade wet-dry sandpaper
Matt acrylic varnish

This combination of colours is exuberant and vibrant, and because the colours have a similar tonal value – they have all been tinted with white – they mix well without disturbing the eye. In this technique a series of parallel lines is obtained without having to repeatedly measure and mark. By masking the whole surface the butted-up tape can simply be removed for painting and the stripe remasked as necessary.

1 Apply the base coat with a roller. Use a chalk line to mark the first vertical, then mask up your stripes, butting the masking tape up across the whole surface and using varying widths of tape. To detack the tape slightly, brush the tacky side across a cotton fabric.

2 Remove one or more strips of masking tape, depending on the width you want the stripe to be.

3 Load a roller with pink matt emulsion paint and apply to the area where the tape has been removed. Remove a strip of tape a little away from the first to roller the second colour, yellow, without risk of smudging.

4 To paint a lilac stripe adjacent to the previously painted lines, wait for the paint to dry, then reapply strips of masking tape over the edges of the dry paint. Roll on the paint. You may want to use a plumbline to ensure you have a true vertical. Let dry.

5 Continue removing and replacing tape to complete the desired number of stripes. Leave to dry.

6 Lightly sand the stripes with fine-grade wet-dry sandpaper to soften the edges. Protect by applying matt acrylic varnish with a paintbrush.

# Roller patterning

## Materials and Equipment

(Pre-cut) foam radiator roller
and tray
Permanent marker pen,
craft knife
Off-white matt emulsion paint
for the base coat
Matt emulsion paints: red,
orange, yellow, brown
Matt acrylic glaze
Household paintbrush
Paint kettle
Decorator's sponge
Detergent

This simple technique results in a complex effect with a vibrant mix of colours and shapes. The finish can be varied by experimenting with the strength of paint-to-glaze mix – more glaze will give a transparency to the paint that means some colours act as a background texture, although still with a strong, graphic pattern. It is important to use a foam roller so that the cut-out shapes retain the paint well and the edges stay clean.

1 Go to an art-supply store and buy a pre-cut, stamp-effect, mini roller. Or make your own: use a permanent marker pen to outline shapes on a mini foam roller. Cut around the shapes with a craft knife so that they stand out to a height of about 1 cm (⅜ inch). Use a large roller if painting a wide area.

2 Apply the base coat with a paintbrush. Mix 1 part red matt emulsion paint to 3 parts matt acrylic glaze. Use a sponge to colourwash the surface (see pages 44–45). Alternatively, you can apply a solid coat of red matt acrylic paint as your background colour.

3 Load the adapted roller with orange matt emulsion paint and use either one clean, straight stroke to apply the paint and pattern, or roll the roller back and forth twice over the area. Continue to cover the whole surface and leave to dry.

4 Wash out the roller and paint tray with detergent and water. Apply a yellow pattern, using the same clean stroke to keep the shapes clear. The first colour will appear as a background echoing the pattern. Allow to dry.

5 Follow Steps 3–4 with brown paint. This final, deeper colour can be diluted with 3 parts matt acrylic glaze to make it more transparent. Let dry.

6 Mix equal amounts of red matt emulsion paint and matt acrylic glaze. Wash this over the surface to soften the colours and give a protective seal.

# Roller spots

## Materials and Equipment

Cream matt emulsion paint for
the base coat

Matt emulsion paints: pale
cream, lilac, light brown,
mid-brown

Matt acrylic glaze

Rollers and trays: mini foam,
mini medium-pile, medium
household rollers

Fine paintbrush, household
paintbrush

Fine-grade wet-dry sandpaper

Detergent

This technique is ideal for decorating a room or
furniture quickly, introducing pattern and colour without
the need for any great skill. As long as the roller end is
not overloaded, the result should be a neat and crisp
application of coloured spots in a random pattern.
Consider the density of spots – too many may make a
small area appear busy – but keep the colours light and
harmonious and the finish will not be overwhelming.

1 Apply the base coat with a roller. Dab the solid end of a mini foam roller in pale cream matt emulsion paint. Dab off the excess. Lightly press the paint-loaded end onto the surface and cleanly remove. Continue to create a random pattern of spots. Leave to dry.

2 Dab the end of a smaller, medium-pile roller in lilac matt emulsion paint. Dab off excess paint then press the roller in the centre of a cream spot. Add lilac inner spots to some of the cream spots, aiming to evenly balance the distribution. Leave to dry. Clean the roller well with detergent and water.

3 Using a clean medium-pile roller, randomly apply smaller light brown spots to some of the cream spots. If the colours appear too dark, add a small amount of matt acrylic glaze to make the paint more transparent.

4 Add mid-brown spots to the remaining circles. Aim for a balanced yet random mix of colours.

5 If some colours appear too dominant you can highlight the centre with a dot of cream matt emulsion paint using a fine paintbrush. Leave to dry.

6 Sand the pattern lightly with fine-grade wet-dry sandpaper to give a smooth finish and apply matt acrylic glaze with a household paintbrush.

# Ragging

## Materials and Equipment

Pale cream matt emulsion
  paint for the base coat
Colourwash mixes:
  stone, ochre
Roller and tray
Household paintbrushes,
  stippling brush
Lint-free cloth
Matt acrylic glaze

This is a relatively easy way to add a little texture to a flat colour without changing the overall appearance greatly. It is best to practise using this technique with lighter colours; you can experiment with colour mixing on a wider scale when you are more confident. The texture created lends itself to large-scale application, and because the cloth is held in a palm-sized pad, the finish is easily and quickly achieved.

1 *Apply the base coat with a roller. Use a paintbrush to apply stone colourwash mix in broad, even strokes in all directions.*

2 *Dab the bristles of a stippling brush into the wet colourwash to remove tiny spots of colour. Work quickly and aim for an even coverage.*

3 *Wad up a pad of slightly damp, lint-free cloth and dab it over the colourwash, lifting off some colour. Work quickly before the glaze has time to dry. Prepare a few pieces of cloth beforehand and discard saturated cloth as necessary. Allow to dry.*

4 *Repeat the whole process with ochre colourwash mix, or redo the stone to achieve a deeper colour before applying the ochre. Leave to dry.*

5 *Any areas that appear too subtle can be treated again by dabbing them over with a cloth dampened with colourwash mix, adding extra colour and texture where required. Allow to dry.*

6 *Finish by applying matt acrylic glaze with a household paintbrush for protection.*

# Overlaying colours

## Materials and Equipment

Dark cream matt emulsion
paint for the base coat
Matt emulsion paints: dark
peach, light peach
Roller and tray
Mutton cloth
Household paintbrush
Matt acrylic glaze

This is a favourite with decorators because it is easy to execute but results in a complex build-up of colours with a soft, even texture. The mutton-cloth weave is loose but regular and therefore allows colour blending to work in a delicate and interesting way. The dark and light peach mix evokes a warm, cosy atmosphere, while the cream adds fresh highlights. This effect can be used with good results on an imperfect surface.

1 Apply the base coat with a roller. Dab a scrunched-up mutton-cloth pad into dark peach matt emulsion paint and remove the excess. Dab the cloth lightly over the surface. Try to work evenly, picking up any excess and redabbing it until dry.

2 Use a clean piece of cloth to apply light peach paint in the same way. The colours can be blended at this stage but do not cover the first colour too much. A large pad of cloth will leave an obvious mark, whereas a small pad will produce a tighter, more controlled texture.

3 When the paint is completely dry, add some of the dark cream base colour to increase the texture and soften any areas that appear too dense with colour. Leave to dry.

4 Work over the area again with the dark peach to add shape to the finish. You could try a cloud effect or a fade from dark to light. On a wall, try darker corners moving into a lighter centre. Let dry.

5 Use a clean piece of cloth to add final touches of light peach to create highlights.

6 Protect by applying matt acrylic glaze, working evenly with regular, short brushstrokes.

# Spray paint and fabric patterning

## Materials and Equipment

White matt emulsion paint for
  the base coat
Open-weave nylon
  netting fabric
Scissors, spray adhesive
Protective face mask
  and gloves
Acrylic spray paints: green,
  blue, silver, light bronze
Roller and tray
Fine-grade wet-dry sandpaper
Beeswax
Lint-free cloth

Nylon fabric can be used as a means of masking a surface from spray paint. Pieces are moved around and the spray paint repeatedly misted over them until the whole surface has received a fine coat of sprayed colour. The shapes of the cut fabric will be lightly outlined as each layer is built up. The rough edges of the fabric allow the paint to meet in a broken edge, helping the colours and shapes to blend gently.

1 Apply the base coat with a roller. Using scissors, cut out random-sized pieces of open-weave nylon netting fabric, leaving the edges uneven. The loose weave will allow some spray paint to pass through and give a light misting of each colour.

2 Before placing the fabric on the surface to be decorated, lay it on a work surface and spray one side of each piece with spray adhesive.

3 Place the fabric pieces, glue-side down, on the surface to be decorated, in a random pattern with some overlapping. Working in a well-ventilated area, wearing a mask and gloves, spray the whole surface lightly with green acrylic spray paint, following the manufacturer's instructions. Leave to dry.

4 Move the fabric and repeat the process with the other spray colours, allowing drying time between each colour. The build-up of layers should be subtle and show a dappling effect like light on water. Stronger colours, like bronze, may be used sparingly in areas that are too subtle.

5 Remove the fabric and, when you are happy with the effect, allow to dry before sanding the surface with fine-grade wet-dry sandpaper to soften.

6 Protect the effect with beeswax, applied with a lint-free cloth and buffed to a sheen.

# Lace stencil

## Materials and Equipment

Taupe matt emulsion paint for
the base coat
Selection of lace-edged cotton
Tape measure, pencil, scissors,
spray adhesive
Protective face mask
and gloves
Acrylic spray paints:
light brown, white
Roller and tray

Lace can be used as a positive stencil for small areas
such as tabletops, curtain pelmets or borders around a
window or floor. You could pick a design that echoes a
fabric decoration in the room. To use the stencil for
repeats or a large area you should stretch the lace on a
metal or wooden frame. Coating the lace with a varnish
or PVA or white glue ensures that it remains flat, and
enables you to use it more than once.

1 *Apply the base coat with a roller. You could also drag the background (see pages 60–61), as here. Measure and mark with a pencil where you want the fabric to be placed. Using a pair of scissors, cut the lace-edged fabric where necessary.*

2 *Place the lace on a work surface and spray the back with spray adhesive. Leave to dry for a few minutes.*

3 *Carefully lay the lace in position, glue side down. When it is as straight as possible, press it lightly into place. Some adhesives allow for repositioning, which is useful if the fabric stretches unevenly.*

4 *Working in a well-ventilated area and wearing a mask and gloves, spray light brown acrylic spray paint directly above the stencil to give a solid, even cover, following the manufacturer's instructions. Leave to dry.*

5 *To spray a white highlight that will make the pattern look more three-dimensional, angle the spray from one side only, so that the white takes to just one side of the pattern. Leave it to dry.*

6 *Carefully remove the lace and clean off any visible pencil marks. The decoration can be misted over with a very light coat of white spray.*

# Muslin frottage

## Materials and Equipment

White eggshell paint for the
  base coat
Pieces of muslin cut to
  approximately 60 cm
  (2 foot) square
PVA or white glue
Colourwash mixes: taupe, blue
Rollers and trays
Matt acrylic glaze
Household paintbrush

The frottage technique involves rubbing a textured
material into wet paint and results in a loose, irregular
texture. In this project it has been combined with
applied colour. The muslin fabric used has a wide
weave that allows paint to pass through and an
absorbency that, if used quickly, will pick up colour
when it is pressed on a wet surface. This texturing can
be used as a background for further decoration.

1 Apply the base coat with a roller. Brush a coat of PVA or white glue over both sides of some muslin fabric and let dry. Pour taupe colourwash mix into a roller tray and coat the roller thoroughly. On a separate surface, roll an even layer of colourwash over one side of the muslin.

2 Lay the muslin on the white surface, paint side down. Use a dry roller to press the muslin onto the surface. The roller pressure will cause the colourwash to transfer to the base and remove any excess.

3 Prepare a second sheet of muslin and coat with blue colourwash mix. Loosely lay the muslin over the frottaged area so some material overlaps and forms subtle folds.

4 Use the dry roller to press the muslin and transfer the colour, as before. Clean the roller every now and then to stop it becoming clogged.

5 Continue building up layers using fresh pieces of scrim. To intensify the effect, lay down the muslin in various states of folding and overlapping. Make sure the colours do not become muddy.

6 Another variation is to apply the colourwash directly to the surface, lay the muslin over it, roller, so that the muslin lifts off some colour, and remove. Protect by applying matt acrylic glaze.

# Textured
## effects

There are many ways to impart texture to a surface. Substances such as all-purpose fillers, metal, mica, and sand can be added to paint to build up texture in the first application. Real plaster and painted stone effects impart character and a sense of history to a new or blank space, or they can add weight and permanence to a flimsy surface. Traditional techniques, such as using gesso and clay plastering, are demonstrated in this chapter alongside novel faux finishes such as imitation suede and slate. Most faux finishes have been devised for use in areas where the real material is inappropriate or will prove too expensive. It is often also impossible to obtain exactly the right colour to suit your needs, therefore a painted imitation may solve many decorative problems. The use of decorative paper to add pattern, texture and colour offers up an endless array of options. The basic materials are cheap and so flexible they can be applied to almost any surface if it is prepared well and sealed with the appropriate varnish. In fact, in the case of craquelure, even varnish can be used to create texture.

When you have experimented with the various techniques, it should be possible for you to use these projects as a guide and begin attempting your own effects. Experimenting with colour variations and combinations of different textures can result in a fascinating range of unique effects, while the multitude of protective glazes and varnishes that is now available allows even the most delicate decoration to be sealed and preserved for some time.

# Sandstone

## Materials and Equipment

Pale cream matt emulsion
  paint for the base coat
Cream, fine-textured, exterior
  housepaint
Acrylic paints: burnt umber,
  yellow ochre
All-purpose filler
Paint kettles
Decorator's sponges
Fitch brush, dusting brush, nail
  brush, household paintbrush
Strip of straight-edged card
Fine- and medium-grade
  wet-dry sandpaper

This effect can be used to add textural interest to any well-prepared surface – a fireplace, a wall or even a piece of furniture – suggesting the permanence and weight of real stone at a fraction of the cost. It can be adapted as required, for a strong or subtle colouration, simply by adding more washes and spattered paint and sanding between coats.

1 *Apply the base coat with a paintbrush. Dab a sponge in the exterior housepaint and remove the excess. Use the sponge to stipple the paint over the surface. Use a fitch brush for recesses and corners. Leave to dry.*

2 *Add a small amount of burnt umber acrylic paint to the exterior housepaint. Mix 1 part filler with 3 parts paint and stir well. Use the sponge to stipple this all over, leaving some areas with the thick mix raised in peaks.*

3 *When the paint is semi-dry, drag a strip of card over the surface, flattening some areas by knocking off the stippled peaks. Leave to dry.*

4 *Dilute burnt umber and yellow ochre acrylic paints 1 part each to 3 parts water. Use a sponge to wash on and wipe away the paints, leaving a build-up of colour in the recesses (see page 51). Let dry. Lightly sand with medium-grade wet-dry sandpaper.*

5 *Dust the surface with a dusting brush. Dilute 1 part pale cream matt emulsion paint to 3 parts water and use a sponge to wash this on all over, enhancing the stone effect and adding depth to the texture.*

6 *Dilute the acrylic colours slightly. Dip a nail brush into the paint, pull back the bristles, and lightly spatter the colour, to suggest the variety of stone. When dry, sand with fine-grade wet-dry sandpaper.*

# Slate

## Materials and Equipment

Mid-tone grey matt emulsion
  paint for the base coat
Dark grey matt emulsion paint
Acrylic paints: dark blue, black
Matt acrylic glaze
Roller and tray
Paint kettle
Household paintbrushes
Medium- and fine-grade
  wet-dry sandpaper
Black shoe polish
Lint-free cloths

This effect recreates the dark grey finish of roof slates, and may be applied to any surface where you might consider using actual slate if it weren't for factors such as cost and weight. By protecting the finish with a few thin coats of glaze or varnish the fake slate may actually last longer than real slate, which is very porous and chips easily.

1 Apply the base coat with a roller. Finish by sanding the top coat with medium- and then fine-grade wet-dry sandpaper. The surface should have as smooth a finish as possible so that the dragged colour can be pulled across easily.

2 Use a paintbrush to apply a coat of dark grey matt emulsion paint, using random brushstrokes. Before the paint dries, drag the brush through it in one direction to give a solid graining effect. When using such dark colours you may want to wear gloves. Leave the paint to dry.

3 Mix dark blue and black acrylic paints to make a blue-black. Mix 1 part blue-black paint to 1 part matt acrylic glaze and 2 parts water. Use a paintbrush to drag the dilute glaze on in the same direction as the dark grey paint.

4 Before the glaze has dried, wipe over the surface with a lint-free cloth, pulling the cloth in the same direction as the previous paint and glaze coats.

5 Use a cloth to apply a thin layer of black shoe polish, again working in the same direction as the previous layers.

6 Buff the surface with a clean, lint-free cloth. The black polish finish can be regularly buffed with a soft cloth and periodically repolished to protect the surface against water damage or staining.

# Terracotta

## Materials and Equipment

Off-white matt emulsion paint
  for the base coat
Tape measure, pencil,
  masking tape
Matt emulsion paints:
  terracotta, grey
Burnt sienna acrylic paint
Textured wall finish
Matt acrylic glaze
Paint kettles
Trowel or large filler knife
Fine-grade wet-dry sandpaper
Decorator's sponge
Fitch brush, household
  paintbrush

This technique can be used as a solid block, without the mortar lines, but should be worked in regular-sized areas so the textured paint can be easily trowelled. The mix cannot be stored for long before it begins to harden, so when working over a large area it's best to mix up small batches as you go. Keep a damp cloth over the mix between uses and retain a colour sample for reference.

1 Apply the base coat with a paintbrush. Use a tape measure and pencil to mark a brick pattern on the wall. Allow a narrow mortar line between each brick.

2 Mask the mortar lines with masking tape. Tear the tape's edges a little to give an uneven edge.

3 Mix a light terracotta textured finish using terracotta matt emulsion paint and textured wall finish (see page 18). Load some of the mix onto a trowel or large filling knife and pull it over the surface. Apply the plaster thinly and do not try to smooth it. Pull quickly in one direction. Leave to dry.

4 If you wish to build up further layers of textured finish, leave it to dry overnight before recoating. If the surface is too rough, lightly sand with fine-grade wet-dry sandpaper before removing the masking tape. Slowly pull the tape off to avoid chipping the edges of the bricks.

5 Mix 1 part burnt sienna acrylic paint to 2 parts matt acrylic glaze. Use a sponge to wash this mix all over the surface. Always leave the textured finish for a few hours before adding any colourwashes. Leave to dry.

6 Use grey matt emulsion paint to mix a textured paint in mortar colour and use a fitch brush to paint in the mortar lines. They can be quite uneven. Do not wash excess textured finish down the drain because it will block it. Rinse tools in a bucket and sieve out solid waste for disposal.

# Stone blockwork

## Materials and Equipment

Cream matt emulsion paint for
the base coat
Tape measure, pencil, thin
masking tape, craft knife
Burnt umber acrylic paint
All-purpose filler
Paint kettles
Rollers and trays
Household paintbrush
Sponge
Medium- and fine-grade
wet-dry sandpaper

The warmth and solidity of mock stone blockwork can be used to great effect in areas that lack character and interest, and it has a soft, smooth texture to the touch. It is also possible to experiment with rollers that have different pile lengths to achieve a tighter or looser texture. The stonework lines should be neat and regular, and it is a good idea to begin marking out in the centre of the area to be decorated.

1 Apply the base coat with a paintbrush. Make sure the surface is free of dust and grease. Use a tape measure and pencil to mark a pattern of blocks to fit inside the chosen space.

2 Use thin masking tape to mask over the pencil lines. Cut the tape neatly with a craft knife where it overlaps into a brick.

3 Add burnt umber acrylic paint to cream matt emulsion paint to mix a mid-brown. Paint a test area and allow to dry to check the true colour. Mix 1 part all-purpose filler to 3 parts mid-brown paint and stir well. Use a roller to apply the first coat. Leave to dry.

4 Follow Step 3, using less burnt umber acrylic paint, to mix a slightly lighter textured brown. Use a roller to apply a solid, even layer. Leave to dry. Do not wash excess filler down the drain because it will block it.

5 To remove the tape, start at one end and pull the tape back against itself slowly. Aim to keep the lines crisp. This will show the cream base colour as the grouting line.

6 Use medium- then fine-grade wet-dry sandpaper to rub down the surface. This will cause the darker background brown to speckle the surface. Wipe over with a damp sponge to remove the dust. Repeat as necessary.

# Limestone paving

## Materials and Equipment

Cream matt emulsion paint for
  the base coat
Tape measure, pencil
Matt emulsion paints: pale
  cream, white
Acrylic paints: yellow ochre,
  burnt umber
Matt acrylic glaze
All-purpose filler
Textured wall finish
Paint kettles
Decorator's sponge
Household and fitch brushes
Medium- and fine-grade
  wet-dry sandpaper

This effect can be used over any well-prepared surface, but is particularly successful on a floor as long as it is well protected, although some wear will add to the character of the finish. The colours shown here are for guidance only, and you may prefer to match the effect to an existing scheme. If you want to imitate a real stone, find a sample of the original to work from.

1 *Apply the base coat with a paintbrush. Mix 1 part all-purpose filler to 3 parts pale cream matt emulsion paint. Then mix 1 part textured wall finish to 3 parts coloured filler. Use a sponge to stipple the mix over the whole surface. Leave the paint stippled with peaks. Let dry.*

2 *Use a tape measure and pencil to mark a pattern of blocks to fit inside the designated space.*

3 *Mix yellow ochre acrylic paint and white matt emulsion paint to produce a warm yellow. Mix 1 part filler to 3 parts paint and stipple it on with a sponge. Let dry. Do not wash excess filler or textured paint down the drain because it will block it.*

4 *Mix 1 part burnt umber acrylic paint to 2 parts matt acrylic glaze and use a fitch brush to paint in the gaps between the blocks. Paint just a few lines at a time and use a sponge to wash the glaze onto the edges of each stone.*

5 *Sand well with medium- then fine-grade wet-dry sandpaper. Dust off and wipe over with a damp sponge to check the final colour and texture. Repeat any of the steps if necessary.*

6 *Mix pale cream matt emulsion paint with a little acrylic glaze and use a sponge to highlight each stone with patches here and there.*

# Imitation leather

## Materials and Equipment

Pale cream matt emulsion
  paint for the base coat
Matt emulsion paints:
  mid-brown, light brown
Burnt umber acrylic paint
All-purpose filler
Paint kettles
Medium-pile rollers and trays
Household paintbrushes
Rag
Fine chisel or gouge
Fine-grade wet-dry sandpaper
Beeswax
Lint-free cloth

The leather effect is created by building up a depth of textured paint, then incising marks through it to suggest the wear and creases of real hide. This finish works wonderfully on walls, furniture and even on thick paper or card to suggest laminated panels. The all-purpose filler thickens the paint and provides a smooth, soft feel when sanded, while the wax finish adds a luxurious feel as well as protection.

1 *Apply the base coat with a paintbrush. Mix 1 part all-purpose filler with 2 parts mid-brown matt emulsion paint. This thick paint should be the consistency of double cream. Apply this in a thick layer with a medium-pile roller. Allow to dry.*

2 *Dilute the mix made up in Step 1 with a little water, to the consistency of single cream. Roll on a smooth layer, covering the first coat completely. Leave to dry.*

3 *Follow Step 1 to mix light brown matt emulsion paint and filler. Dab it on with a paintbrush then smooth off with a wet rag, combining smooth and textured areas. Leave to dry. Do not wash excess filler down the drain because it will block it.*

4 *Use a small chisel or gouge to scratch lines to imitate the creases of leather hide. These should be uneven, broken lines, not straight or parallel. Do not dig too deep. Sand lightly all over with fine-grade wet-dry sandpaper until the surface feels smooth.*

5 *Dilute 1 part burnt umber acrylic paint to 2 parts water. Wash this mix all over with a brush. Leave to dry, then repeat the wash until you have reached the desired depth of colour. Allow to dry.*

6 *Use a lint-free cloth to apply a layer of beeswax and buff to a soft sheen.*

# Imitation snakeskin

## Materials and Equipment

Acrylic primer
Snakeskin source, pencil,
    tracing paper, craft knife,
    cutting mat, masking tape
Manila stencil card
Matt emulsion paints: cream,
    dark cream
Burnt umber acrylic paint
All-purpose filler
Paint kettles
Decorator's sponge
Hog-hair softening brush, fitch
    brush, household paintbrush
Fine-grade wet-dry sandpaper
Matt acrylic glaze

This effect demonstrates how easy it is to achieve a complex decoration using just one stencil worked over repeatedly. Hand cutting stencils is a labour of love and very tiring, but well worth the effort for a truly individual result. The decoration can appear very dramatic and theatrical, adding an intriguing pattern to a tabletop or cupboard. On walls it is better to limit the effect to one wall or borders.

1 *Draw a snakeskin design on tracing paper. Turn the paper over and scribble with pencil over the back of the design. Turn the paper over again, lay it on a sheet of stencil card, and redraw the design to imprint it onto the card. Leave a border all around.*

2 *Use a craft knife over a cutting mat to carefully cut out the stencil. Always use a sharp blade and try to follow all the shapes that can be cut from one side before turning the card to cut the others.*

3 *Prime and sand the surface using a paintbrush, acrylic primer and fine-grade wet-dry sandpaper. Mix 1 part all-purpose filler with 3 parts cream matt emulsion paint. Sponge on the thickened paint and leave to dry. Do not wash excess filler down the drain because it will block it.*

4 *Fix the stencil in place with masking tape and draw around the corners with pencil for repositioning later. Stipple dark cream matt emulsion paint through the cut areas of the stencil with a hog-hair brush. Do not build a solid layer of paint. Remove the stencil to check the effect and lightly sand.*

5 *Reposition the stencil. Dilute 1 part burnt umber acrylic paint with 2 parts matt acrylic glaze and use a fitch brush to apply darker details over the stencil. Add highlights using cream emulsion paint.*

6 *Remove the stencil and allow the paint to dry. Apply matt acrylic glaze with a household paintbrush to seal and protect.*

# Denim effect

## Materials and Equipment

Scissors
Hessian
PVA or white glue
Pale blue matt emulsion paint
Denim blue colourwash mix
Household paintbrush,
  dragging brush
Rollers and trays
Fine-grade wet-dry sandpaper
Cloth for cleaning
Matt acrylic glaze

The hessian-textured background gives an interesting, worn appearance to this painted denim look. The effect is quite dark so it should be used sparingly, limited to one wall, perhaps, or saved for details. It is a great technique to use for revamping old furniture. The effect can also be adapted in many ways: the dragging could be made much broader, for example, or you could introduce another colour.

1 Cut out manageable-sized squares of hessian with a pair of scissors. Coat with a mix of 1 part PVA or white glue to 2 parts water and let dry. Make sure the surface is dust and grease free. Roll on a very thick layer of pale blue matt emulsion paint. Leave for just a few minutes.

2 Press a prepared piece of hessian into the wet paint. Rub over the back of the fabric with a dry roller to make an impression in the paint. Remove the hessian. When dry, lightly sand with fine-grade wet-dry sandpaper to lift any hessian hairs.

3 Use a paintbrush to apply denim blue colourwash mix in an even layer. Use a dragging brush to drag vertical lines through the wash, removing some of the colour. Turn the brush over repeatedly and clean by wiping onto a damp cloth regularly.

4 While the colourwash is still slightly wet, use the dragging brush to pull the colour in a horizontal direction to help suggest the weave of the fabric.

5 Use fine-grade wet-dry sandpaper to lightly sand the surface and reveal the broken texture of the base paint. This will give the effect of worn denim.

6 Protect the effect by applying matt acrylic glaze with a household paintbrush.

# Imitation moiré silk

## Materials and Equipment

Pale blue matt emulsion paint
for the base coat
Mid-blue colourwash mix
Roller and tray
Household paintbrushes,
hog-hair softening brush,
flogging brush
Heartgrainer
Rubber comb
Fine-grade wet-dry sandpaper
Cloth for cleaning
Satin acrylic varnish

The painted imitation of moiré silk must have the same fine finish as the original, so just one colour is used, keeping the tones of base paint and glaze coat very similar. In this way the pattern is merely hinted at, rather then appearing overbearing. Combining it with other subtle effects, such as stippling and graining, will ensure it retains its luxurious finish. This effect can look stunning if completed in an opalescent finish.

1 Apply the base coat with a roller. Sand lightly using fine-grade wet-dry sandpaper for a completely smooth finish. Use a paintbrush to apply an even coat of mid-blue colourwash mix. While the wash is still wet, drag the brush through in regular vertical strokes. Turn the brush over regularly and clean with a damp cloth when saturated with paint.

2 While the colourwash is still wet, pull a heartgrainer through, starting from one end and working in a regular vertical direction. Pull slowly and gently pivot the tool in a rocking motion so that the effect of woodgrain appears.

3 Drag a rubber comb through the wet wash to create vertical stripes in some areas.

4 Use a hog-hair softening brush over the whole area to smooth the effect. Follow the direction of the previous strokes.

5 When the glaze is almost dry, use a flogging brush to pull it in a vertical direction again. This will add more suggestion of the weave.

6 Use the softening brush to pull the lines in a horizontal direction and enhance the suggestion of the weave of the fabric. Leave to dry and apply satin acrylic varnish with a household paintbrush.

# Imitation suede panelling

## Materials and Equipment

Pale cream matt emulsion
  paint for the base coat
Tape measure, pencil,
  plumbline, masking tape,
  craft knife
Matt emulsion paints:
  mid-brown, light brown
Burnt umber acrylic paint
Matt acrylic glaze
All-purpose filler
Paint kettles
Medium-pile rollers and trays
Decorator's sponge
Household paintbrush
Fine-grade wet-dry sandpaper

This understated effect has a tactile as well as visual appeal: run your hand over the surface and you can feel how similar to stretched suede the sanded paint-and-filler mix is. A thick paint applied with a medium-pile roller creates the illusion of the subtle pile of suede. Washes of colour then add depth and interest to the finish. Finally, light sanding takes the peaks off the textured paint until it shows through the washes.

1 *Apply the base coat with a roller. Mix 1 part all purpose filler with 2 parts mid-brown matt emulsion paint. Roll at least two coats of the lightly textured paint mix as evenly as possible over the whole area with a medium-pile roller. Leave to dry.*

2 *Mix filler and light brown matt emulsion paint as in Step 1 and roll on evenly. Leave to dry. Do not wash excess filler down the drain because it will block it.*

3 *Measure and mark out panels with a pencil, according to the size of area being treated. Use a plumbline to get your first vertical.*

4 *Mask alternate panels. On textured paint the tape may not stick down easily, so check the adhesion before painting.*

5 *Mix 1 part burnt umber acrylic paint with 2 parts matt acrylic glaze and use a sponge to apply it to each alternate panel. Use a brush to form a darker edge near the tape, feathering the colour out into the main panel. Leave to dry.*

6 *Remove the masking tape and use fine-grade wet-dry sandpaper to lightly sand the panels. Seal with matt acrylic glaze using a household paintbrush. Leave to dry.*

# Stucco

## Materials and Equipment

Sealed board for mixing
plaster, knife
Plaster sealant
Rose white matt emulsion
paint for the base coat
Ready-made stucco plaster
Burnt sienna liquid pigment
Paint kettles
Household paintbrush
Plasterer's hawk and trowel,
filling knife
Cloth for cleaning
Medium-grade wet-dry
sandpaper

In this finish the warm terracotta shade of fresh plaster is imbued with the sensuous softness and sheen of polished stucco. Stucco has a harder finish than ordinary plaster, yet it is quick and easy to repair as long as samples of colour and mixing ratios for the pigment are recorded when it is first used. Keep the plaster mix under a damp cloth and carry a small amount to work with.

1 *Follow the manufacturer's instructions for colouring the stucco. Mix the burnt sienna liquid pigment and ready-made stucco plaster on a sealed board using a knife. Always mix small amounts, checking the colour against a sample to retain consistency. Use a cloth to clean up at every stage. Wear protective gloves.*

2 *Apply the base coat with a paintbrush. Use a brush to apply a thin glaze of plaster sealant. Leave to dry. Apply the first coat of coloured stucco, using a plasterer's hawk and trowel for large areas or a filling knife for smaller patches. Pull the plaster thinly and evenly across the surface. Allow to dry.*

3 *Dampen some medium-grade wet-dry sandpaper and wipe a steel filling knife across the surface in a circular motion. Keep the blade at a shallow angle. This will sharpen the blade and soften the edges.*

4 *Apply a second layer of the same plaster mix. Apply it in a series of thin layers with the filling knife. Use a continuous motion, pulling and wiping the plaster, changing direction regularly. Clean and rebevel the knife often.*

5 *Continue adding thin plaster layers. As the surface becomes more solid, lower the angle of the knife and use it to polish the plaster with a circular motion, taking care not to scratch it.*

6 *As the steel slides over the plaster any raised lines on the surface will disappear and the matt plaster will take on a glossy sheen.*

# Rustic clay

## Materials and Equipment

Cream matt emulsion paint for
  the base coat
Clay plaster
Craft knife
Scrim
Tape measure
PVA or white glue
Paint kettles
Household paintbrushes
Plasterer's hawk and trowel
Decorator's sponge
Fine-grade wet-dry sandpaper

Clay plasters have been developed to take account of the needs of the modern user and the natural environment, and today's products are both ecologically sound and easy to use. The plaster, in powder form to be mixed with water, has a soft, matt, chalky finish. It is breathable and can assist in regulating indoor humidity. Colours are limited since clay can only be obtained in natural shades.

1 Apply the base coat with a paintbrush. Adding scrim to the surface will help the adhesion of the clay plaster. Measure up the area to be plastered and cut pieces of scrim into manageable-sized squares to seal the surface.

2 Dilute 1 part PVA or white glue with 2 parts water and brush over the surface. Apply the scrim and paint over with more of the dilute glue until completely adhered. Leave to dry.

3 Follow the manufacturer's guidelines for mixing the clay plaster and water. It is important to try sample areas of varying thicknesses to allow you to make the preferred choice of finish.

4 Dip a wet paintbrush into the clay mix and apply a thin wash over the scrim. Leave to dry.

5 Use a plasterer's hawk and trowel to apply a more substantial layer of clay plaster. Do not wash excess plaster down the drain because it will block it.

6 While the mix is drying, smooth the surface by wiping over it with a damp sponge. Leave to dry and sand with fine-grade wet-dry sandpaper. If using more than one colour, let the first one dry, then apply the second, blending them at the meeting point.

# Aged plaster effect

## Materials and Equipment

Pale cream matt emulsion
   paint for the base coat
Terracotta colourwash mix
Off-white matt emulsion paint
Yellow ochre acrylic paint
Matt acrylic glaze
Finishing plasters: grey, white
Roller and tray
Paint kettles
Decorator's sponge
Plasterer's hawk and trowel
Filling knife
Cloth for cleaning
Fine-grade wet-dry sandpaper

Use this technique to introduce a theatrical element to your interior: perfectly finished walls acquire instant character using this dramatic aging effect. Finishing plasters can be bought in light grey or white and are transparent when wet, and opaque when dry. Colour can either be added to the plaster mix or applied as a final coat. The plaster is then sealed with a matt acrylic glaze for protection.

1 Apply the base coat with a roller. Use a sponge to wash on terracotta colourwash in a figure-of-eight motion. Leave to dry.

2 Mix equal amounts of off-white matt emulsion paint and matt acrylic glaze and apply as in Step 1. Leave to dry.

3 Mix up grey finishing plaster following the manufacturer's instructions. Use a plasterer's hawk and trowel to apply a thin, irregular layer, leaving the base colours to show through in some areas. Clean the trowel with a damp cloth often. Leave to dry.

4 Mix up white finishing plaster as before and apply a thin coat as in Step 3, leaving areas of the base colours and the grey plaster still showing. Leave to dry.

5 Add a little yellow ochre acrylic paint to white finishing plaster to make a cream plaster. Use a filling knife to add patches here and there. The plaster is quite transparent so repeat any of the steps where the finish is too bland and even. Leave to dry.

6 Lightly sand the whole surface with fine-grade wet-dry sandpaper until smooth to the touch. Seal by applying matt acrylic glaze with a household paintbrush.

# Gesso

## Materials and Equipment

Heatproof bowl, mixing bowl
Distilled water
Ready-mixed gesso
Watercolour paints
Household paintbrushes,
  hog-hair brush
Flat metal scraper
Fine-grade wet-dry sandpaper
Lint-free cloths
Beeswax

Gesso leaves a smooth, absorbent surface that is an especially good base for watercolours. The transparency and luminosity of the paints glows through, enlivening the pure white ground. The finish has a cool, smooth feel. It is applied in a series of thin layers that must be taken from the same batch so that the consistency is constant. Gesso is made from rabbit-skin glue and the ready-mixed version only requires warming.

1 *Pour boiling water into a heatproof bowl. Place ready-mixed gesso in a mixing bowl in the water. Keep stirring the gesso until melted to the consistency of single cream.*

2 *Ensure you have as smooth a base as possible, and that it is free of grease and dust. Pour off a little gesso and mix in equal amounts with distilled water. Size the area with the very watery gesso mix. Allow to dry.*

3 *Apply undiluted gesso to the surface using a hog-hair brush. Brush it in well, working in different directions. Apply at least eight coats, adding the next when the previous is matt but not completely dry. Let the final coat dry thoroughly.*

4 *Wet some fine-grade wet-dry sandpaper and sand the surface, keeping a layer of water between it and the gesso. Wipe the surface with a wet cloth to create a 'slurry' of gesso to fill hollows. Leave overnight. Hold a flat metal scraper at an angle and pull it diagonally in one direction then the other to recut the surface. Wipe with a wet cloth. Let dry.*

5 *Brush dilute watercolour paints over the surface, blending the colours with the brush. Repeat as necessary, without muddying the colours. Let dry.*

6 *Add further watercolours and rag the surface with a damp, lint-free cloth. Protect with beeswax, applied and buffed with a soft cloth.*

# Combing

## Materials and Equipment

White matt emulsion paint for
the base coat
Tape measure, pencil,
masking tape
Pale blue matt emulsion paint
Mid-blue colourwash mix
Roller and tray
Household paintbrushes
Grout spreader
Rubber comb
Fine-grade wet-dry sandpaper
Cloth for cleaning
Matt acrylic varnish

The combing technique, when used with a restricted
and subtle colour palette, can give interesting and
sensitive results. Combing can produce many different
patterns, and if the paint is combed thickly, the ridges
formed create the effect of an embossed surface. As
usual, careful planning and application are the keys to
success. Preparation is especially important because
the comb needs a smooth surface to work consistently.

1 *Apply the base coat with a roller. Measure and, with a pencil, mark up the area to be decorated into broad bands.*

2 *Tape the edges of the bands, making sure the masking tape is well adhered to the surface.*

3 *Use a roller to paint alternate bands with pale blue matt emulsion paint. Leave to dry, then lightly sand with fine-grade wet-dry sandpaper to give a smooth surface.*

4 *Use a paintbrush to apply an even coat of mid-blue colourwash mix over the pale blue base.*

5 *While the colourwash is still wet, use a grout spreader to pull thick vertical lines through it. Take care not to lift the masking tape at the edges of the band. Clean the spreader regularly with a damp cloth. Leave to dry.*

6 *Remove the masking tape. Mask the painted bands. In the next strip, follow Steps 4–5, using a commercial rubber comb to create finer stripes. Work horizontally and vertically to form a checked pattern. Leave to dry, then protect with matt acrylic varnish.*

# Stencilling with filler and mica

## Materials and Equipment

Lavender white matt emulsion
   paint for the base coat
Ruler, pencil, masking tape
Simple handmade card stencil
   (see page 99)
Colourwash mixes: lavender,
   blue
Pink acrylic paint
All-purpose filler
Mica flakes
Matt acrylic glaze
Roller and tray; paint kettles
Decorator's sponge
Stencil brush, household
   paintbrushes
Fine-grade wet-dry sandpaper

The addition of all-purpose filler to bulk out plain paint causes it to behave more like a plaster, and the mica flakes give a sparkling glitter. This results in a three-dimensional aspect to simple stencilling. The mica flakes can also be added to solid paint and will glisten on the surface, or sprinkled onto wet glaze if working on a flat surface. The flakes are added as required, so let a sample dry to help you decide how much to use.

1 *Apply the base coat using a roller. Apply a lavender and blue colourwash using a sponge (see pages 44–45). Measure, mark up with a pencil, and mask a border with masking tape.*

2 *Mix 1 part all-purpose filler with 2 parts pink acrylic paint. Position the stencil in the border and hold in place with tape. Use a stencil brush to stipple the thick pink paint through the stencil. Move the stencil on and repeat. Leave to dry.*

3 *Lightly sand the raised decoration with fine-grade wet-dry sandpaper.*

4 *Mix 1 part pink acrylic paint with 2 parts matt acrylic glaze and add a teaspoon of mica flakes. Use a soft brush to wash this glitter colour over the lavender and blue colourwash. Leave to dry.*

5 *Mix a deeper pink glaze by adding more paint to glaze, and include mica flakes as before. Wash this over the stencilled border. Leave to dry.*

6 *Remove the masking tape to reveal the original colourwash base as bands on the edge of the stencil border. Lightly sand the border again to bring out the stencilled textured decoration.*

# Crackle effect

Acrylic primer
Dull green, oil-based
  eggshell paint
Matt emulsion, water-based
  paints: light blue, white
All-purpose / ready-mixed filler
White spirit
Paint kettles
Household paintbrushes,
  thin fitch brush
Hair dryer (or hot air gun)
Medium- and fine-grade
  sandpaper
Lint-free cloth
Matt acrylic glaze or varnish

This finish resembles weathered painted wood and adds tactile as well as visual interest. The crackling effect is due to the different drying speeds of the two paints, while the addition of all-purpose filler to the top coat further speeds up its drying time and helps form a paste that can easily adhere to the eggshell. The emulsion paint sands down to give a smooth finish and is still absorbent to coloured glaze or varnish.

1 Prime and sand the surface with fine-grade wet-dry sandpaper. Use a brush to apply a coat of dull green eggshell base colour. Leave to dry. Sand lightly and apply a second coat, ending with a downwards brushstroke each time to avoid drips.

2 Mix 1 part ready-mixed all-purpose filler with 2 parts light blue matt emulsion paint. Add more filler if necessary to make the mix the consistency of double cream. When the eggshell is touch dry, brush on this mix in quick, even brushstrokes.

3 To assist the drying process and to ensure the crackle glaze effect works as evenly as possible, use a hair dryer (or a hot-air gun if one is available) to warm the paint. Move the heat constantly over the surface, working from a distance of at least 60 cm (2 feet) to prevent possible blistering.

4 Leave to dry thoroughly for at least four hours. The top paint coat will have cracked. Sand with medium-grade sandpaper to remove any roughness from the surface. Wipe off the dust with a dry paintbrush and a damp, lint-free cloth.

5 Add a little white matt emulsion paint to the paint and filler mix and dry brush (see pages 54–55) to add further aging. Leave to dry. Do not wash excess filler down the drain because it will block it.

6 Mix equal amounts of the dull green eggshell and white spirit and use a thin fitch brush to apply this mix to the grooves in places. Leave to dry. Protect with matt acrylic glaze or varnish.

# Craquelure

## Materials and Equipment

Pale cream matt emulsion
    paint for the base coat
Scissors, decoupage designs
PVA or white glue
Two-part craquelure varnish
Artist's oil paint: burnt umber
White spirit
Roller and tray
Paint kettle
Household paintbrushes,
    flat varnishing brushes
Hair dryer or hot-air gun
Lint-free cloth
Matt or eggshell oil varnish

The fine cracks that appear in the top coat of a craquelure varnish only become obvious when colour is rubbed into them, giving an effect reminiscent of the surface of old oil paintings. The two-part varnish – consisting of a slow-drying base coat and a brittle, quick-drying top coat – is an nice way to age colour-work or motifs, especially over a light base. Experiment with thin and thick coats of varnish for the best results.

1 Apply the base coat using a roller. Carefully cut out decoupage designs with scissors and use glue to fix them in place. Leave to dry.

2 Use a flat varnishing brush to apply an even coat of the first part of a two-part craquelure varnish. Leave to dry completely.

3 Take a clean varnishing brush and dampen it slightly. Apply the top coat of the two-part craquelure varnish in an even layer.

4 To assist the drying process and ensure the craquelure works as evenly as possible, use a hair dryer or hot-air gun to warm the varnish. Move the heat constantly over the surface, working from a distance of at least 60 cm (2 feet) (any closer may cause blistering).

5 Dilute 1 part burnt umber oil paint with 2 parts white spirit to make a watery mix. Brush on in a loose scrubbing motion, pushing the colour into all the fine cracks that should have appeared in the varnish. Leave to dry for 15 minutes.

6 Make a pad from a soft lint-free cloth and polish off the oil paint glaze, leaving the colour in the cracks but wiping the surface back to a dirty cream. Leave to dry overnight and protect by applying matt or eggshell oil varnish with a household paintbrush.

# Collage

## Materials and Equipment

Unbleached tissue papers,
  handmade Japanese tissue
  papers, dried pressed leaves
  and flowers, coloured papers
PVA or white glue
Ruler
Household paintbrushes
Dead flat oil varnish
White spirit
Paint kettle

Blending a range of decorative papers, dried plants and tissue papers produces an intricate design of images and colours to transform a bland wall. A final varnish coat not only protects but makes the papers more transparent, unifies the colours and adds depth. The technique is ideal for hiding irregularities, cracks and holes so can be used to disguise unattractive fitted furniture or shelving that cannot be removed.

1 Tear pieces of unbleached and Japanese tissue papers into random sizes. Mix 1 part glue with 2 parts water. Coat the surface with dilute glue. Position the torn paper shapes, and paint over them with glue, working it in well. Overlap the papers to add texture.

2 While the paper is still wet, position dried, pressed leaves and flowers and brush over with glue as before.

3 Prepare torn pieces of tissue paper as in Step 1 and use them to cover the leaves, again brushing over them with more glue solution.

4 Tear strips and random shapes from coloured papers and prepare with dilute glue. Apply these and seal. Use a ruler to apply pressure.

5 Cover the decoration once more with pieces of tissue paper. Leave to dry overnight.

6 Dilute equal amounts of dead flat oil varnish and white spirit and paint over the decoration. Leave to dry, then apply a second coat. The papers will become transparent and the decorations will start to show through the layers.

# Collage and decoupage

## Materials and Equipment

White matt emulsion paint for the base coat
Tape measure, pencil, ruler, scissors
Selection of tissue papers and handmade coloured papers
PVA or white glue
Paint kettle
Household paintbrush
Satin oil varnish

This project combines collage and decoupage and introduces the concept of multi-coloured decoration. Collage is the art of making pictures and decoration by layering papers, whereas decoupage is the process of cutting out and gluing paper images. The long fibres of the handmade papers help make this a long-lasting form of decoration, while the use of tissue paper also ensures that the finish does not become too bulky.

1 *Apply the base coat. Measure the area to be decorated and mark up with evenly spaced squares in a grid.*

2 *Measure and tear against a straight edge squares of tissue papers, slightly larger than the grid squares so that they can be overlaid.*

3 *Using scissors, cut out abstract motifs from an assortment of coloured papers. Arrange these over the tissue-paper squares. Mix equal quantities of glue and water. Use a brush to apply the glue to the motifs and fix in place.*

4 *Use the glue solution to fix the decorated paper squares to alternate squares on the grid.*

5 *Brush glue solution over the remaining alternate decorated papers, overlapping the edges of the previously glued squares. Leave to dry overnight.*

6 *Finish with at least three coats of satin oil varnish, brushing it in well and letting it dry between coats. This will make the papers more transparent as well as protecting the finish.*

# Traditional
## effects

The traditional effects are often more advanced and involved than the finishes described in the previous chapters. Many are cost-effective ways of achieving a glamour and richness within a dull interior or on an object of humble origin. Faux or bravura effects aim to deceive the eye, creating an illusion of a real material like marble or wood. These effects range from fantasy finishes to a perfect deception executed well enough to appear to have the weight and substance of the actual material. When marbling, for example, the decorator can either follow the colours and veining of real marble or experiment with a variety of colours and patterns. If the basic principles are followed, you need be limited only by your imagination.

In most cases, it is recommended that you use oil paints to achieve a convincing faux finish. They not only allow you plenty of time to manipulate the wet glaze and achieve the desired effect, but oil glazes also have a luminosity that is not comparable with modern water-based equivalents. Originally these finishes would have been executed on gesso, which offers a wonderful smooth, cool surface. The modern-day equivalent is an eggshell finish oil- or water-based paint, which also works extremely well if sanded carefully.

Some degree of artistry is required from the painter at this stage and these finishes should be used with careful regard to their impact on the overall room scheme. It is advisable to use them where one might conceive of using the real thing.

# Sienna marble

## Materials and Equipment

White oil-based eggshell paint
  for the base coat
Hog-hair softening brush
Artist's oil paints: raw sienna,
  gold ochre, burnt umber,
  burnt sienna
White spirit
Paint kettles
Roller and tray
Household paintbrushes,
  long-bristled artist's brush
Decorator's sponge
Feather
Mutton cloth
Eggshell oil varnish

This effect aims to capture the essence of marble in paint, rather than produce a facsimile surface. The suggestion of solidity, depth and translucency of real sienna marble is simulated in the glazed layers and soft textures and markings. Oil glazes reproduce the desired translucency and dry slowly, giving you time to manipulate the effect. The base coat of white eggshell paint should imitate the smooth, cool touch of gesso.

1 Apply the base coat with a roller. Mix raw sienna and gold ochre glazes by diluting 1 part oil paint to 3 parts white spirit. Paint the glazes on in broad, diagonal shapes, without mixing the colours. Soften by brushing in all directions with a hog-hair softening brush.

2 To add texture, dip a sponge in white spirit and lightly dab it over the surface. Dip a feather in white spirit and pull it over the surface to add some faint veining. Leave to partially dry, then soften with the softening brush. Allow to dry.

3 Mix 1 part white eggshell paint to 2 parts white spirit and brush this loosely on. Smooth over the glaze with a mutton-cloth pad to remove brushmarks. Finish with the softening brush to ensure smoothness and leave to dry.

4 Mix burnt umber and burnt sienna glazes as in Step 1. Apply in broad directional strokes where the veining will be and soften as in Step 3. When dry, dilute burnt umber oil paint in a little white spirit and use a long-bristled artist's brush or feather to paint in the veins.

5 The veins should not be too distinct or rigid, so soften them with the softening brush, blending the lines with the more subtle layers beneath. Keep adding to and softening the veins, referring to a photographic source if necessary.

6 While the veining dries, load a brush with white spirit and pull back and release the bristles to lightly spatter the surface. Leave to dry. Protect by applying eggshell oil varnish with a household paintbrush.

# Breccia marble

## Materials and Equipment

White eggshell paint for the base coat
Artist's oil paint: raw umber
White spirit
Paint kettles
Household paintbrushes, hog-hair softening brush, long-haired sable brush
Lint-free cloth
Eggshell oil varnish

Breccia marble is formed when shattered fragments of mineral are reformed into solid rock, which is why the pattern resembles two-dimensional pebbles. If you consider the design carefully and make sure there is a flow in the pebble patterns, this finish can look realistic in any colour. A contrast in shapes can be achieved by combining sparsely and densely patterned areas.

1 Apply the base coat with a paintbrush. Mix 1 part raw umber oil paint to 2 parts white spirit and brush a thin, even layer of glaze onto the surface.

2 Use a pad of lint-free cloth to wipe out areas of glaze and mark the marble pattern. Vary the size and look of the shapes, with some small and angular and others large, softly rounded, and pebble-like. Remember to leave glaze edges.

3 Soften off the whole surface by brushing over in a variety of directions with a hog-hair softening brush. Leave to dry.

4 Dilute more raw umber oil paint in a little white spirit. Use a long-haired sable brush to paint in the veining lines around the wiped-out shapes. Soften the lines to blend the colour with the background and ensure the veins are not too distinct.

5 Continue adding veins to the outlines, mixing softened, subtle, lighter veins with stronger, angular lines and some very graphic, dark areas. If a shape does not have the desired effect you can clean it off with a rag and start again.

6 Soften all over, again working into some veins more than others. Gently wipe off areas that are too obvious with a soft cloth and a touch of white spirit. Leave to dry. Protect by applying eggshell oil varnish with a household paintbrush.

# Carrara marble

## Materials and Equipment

White oil-based eggshell paint
  for the base coat
Artist's oil paints:
  Payne's grey, Davy's grey,
  alizarin crimson
Oil-based glazing liquid
White spirit
Paint kettles
Household paintbrushes,
  hog-hair softening brush
Feather
Lint-free cloth
Eggshell oil varnish

Carrara marble is generally very understated, with sparse, blurred veins in a clearly forked design. The scale and pattern of veining can be altered to suit the size of the area being decorated: in a small area, for example, the veins can be applied more intensely. The use of three shades of grey, rather than black, gives the marbling a soft appearance, even when veined quite regularly.

1 Apply the base coat with a paintbrush. Mix 1 part oil-based glazing liquid to 2 parts white spirit and brush on until the surface is completely wet.

2 Mix 1 part each of Payne's grey, Davy's grey, and a pale pink-grey mixed from Davy's grey and a little alizarin crimson, with 3 parts white spirit to make three gray glazes. Use a small brush to apply the separate glazes thinly in patches while the glazing liquid is still wet.

3 Blend in the colours by brushing over in a variety of directions with a hog-hair softening brush. Leave to dry.

4 Apply another layer of glazing liquid as in Step 1. Add a little white spirit to Payne's grey oil paint to make it fluid. Use a feather to add grey veining, pulling the length of the feather across the surface to create vague, broken lines.

5 Soften off the veining by brushing gently in different directions with the softening brush. The lines will become blurred.

6 Repeat Steps 4–5 as necessary. Wipe out areas that appear too dark with a lint-free cloth. Leave to dry. Protect by applying eggshell oil varnish.

# Rhodocrosite

## Materials and Equipment

White oil-based eggshell paint
for the base coat
Artist's oil paints: burnt sienna,
alizarin crimson,
yellow ochre
Oil-based glazing liquid
White spirit
Paint kettles
Small household paintbrushes,
hog-hair softening brush
Lint-free cloth
Card
Rubber graining comb
Eggshell oil varnish

Rhodocrosite is a highly coloured manganese-bearing mineral with large pink to blood-red crystals formed in parallel, undulating curved bands varying in width from 6 cm (2½ inches) to tiny pinstripes. The mineral is highly prized and used sparingly, so the painted simulation has traditionally been used for small areas such as borders, tabletops and detailing.

1 *Apply the base coat. Lightly draw curving bands of varying widths. Mix 1 part each of burnt sienna, alizarin crimson, and alizarin crimson with a little yellow ochre to 1 part oil-based glazing liquid. Mix 1 part of each red glaze to 2 parts white spirit. Brush on the red bands in any order.*

2 *Making sure you are wearing protective gloves, use a lint-free cloth to wipe out a few curved ribbons between some of the red bands. You can also wipe the cloth lightly over some bands to thin the colour for a little variety.*

3 *Mix a yellow ochre glaze as in Step 1. Apply to the ribbons where the paint has been wiped back. Allow the colours to bleed into each other.*

4 *Use a torn piece of card to scrape off angled patches of paint from the bands, revealing the white base colour. The sharp edges should be at right angles to the bands of strata. Soften by brushing in all directions with a hog-hair softening brush.*

5 *Gently pull a rubber graining comb through the bands, following the curves. Pull torn pieces of card of different sizes over the bands as with the comb. Replace the card as it becomes saturated.*

6 *Lightly repaint the yellow bands to enhance them and etch faults into the glaze with the side of a piece of card. Soften with repeated strokes of the softening brush. Protect with eggshell oil varnish.*

# Granite

## Materials and Equipment

Grey oil-based eggshell paint
  for the base coat
Artist's oil paints: black, white,
  Davy's grey, Payne's grey
White spirit
Paint kettles
Roller and tray
Household paintbrushes,
  fitch brushes, hog-hair
  softening brush
Decorator's sponges
Lint-free cloth
Eggshell oil varnish

Granite has a coarse texture that can be reproduced in paint by spattering and sponging. When choosing the area or object to paint with this finish, remember that granite is solid looking, and weight and substance are suggested by decorating with this technique. Often the best faux finishes are actually quite simple to achieve and the real art lies in getting the colour mix right, so refer to a sample of the real stone when possible.

1 Apply the base coat with a roller. Mix black and white oil paints to create a black-grey. Combine 1 part black-grey with 2 parts white spirit. Use a brush to evenly wash on the glaze.

2 Soften the wet glaze coat by repeatedly pressing a sponge into it, changing the direction and pressure used regularly.

3 Add a dash of white spirit to Davy's grey oil paint and a pale black-grey mixed from black and white oil paints. Brush the paints onto clean sponges and dab onto the surface. As the colours bleed into each other the blending will add to the texture.

4 Dip a fitch brush in white spirit. Pull back and gently release the bristles to spatter the white spirit over the surface. After a few minutes, dab a sponge all over to add to the granite texture. Soften by dabbing with a lint-free cloth.

5 Spatter the surface with a mix of Payne's grey, Davy's grey, pale black-grey and a dash of white spirit. Leave for a few minutes then dab off as in Step 4.

6 Wait until nearly dry, then repeat any of the steps to build up the effect as necessary. When the finish is tacky, soften by brushing over in a variety of directions with a hog-hair softening brush. Let dry. Protect by applying eggshell oil varnish.

# Oak

## Materials and Equipment

Cream eggshell paint for the
  base coat
Artist's oil paints: raw umber,
  burnt umber, yellow ochre,
  white
White spirit
Paint kettles
Household paintbrushes,
  flogging brush
Rubber comb
Heartgrainer
Lint-free cloth
Cloth for cleaning
Eggshell oil varnish

Oak is one of the easier woods to simulate. Dragging, combing and flogging removes much of the glaze coat which means you can arrive at a subtle copy without the need for softening. The lights added at the end are the most characteristic marks of this particular wood. Real and simulated oak is often used to panel a whole room, and it is therefore a good idea to break up the decoration into panels before you begin painting.

1 *Apply the base coat. Mix raw umber, burnt umber, yellow ochre, and white oil paints to the desired oak shade. Mix 1 part paint with 2 parts white spirit. Brush on the glaze then drag the brush back through it, working in a straight line in one direction.*

2 *Make sure you are wearing protective gloves. Pull a flogging brush through the glaze, working in the same direction as before and keeping as even and straight a line as possible. This will thin the glaze coat.*

3 *Pull a rubber comb through the glaze in the same direction once again. Comb across the whole surface, using the different sides of the comb to vary the effect. Regularly clean the excess glaze from the comb onto a cloth.*

4 *Pull a heartgrainer through the glaze, pivoting it gently at regular intervals. Continue graining, leaving combed strips of varying widths between each grained one. Alter the angle as you rock and pivot the heartgrainer each time for a natural look.*

5 *Comb the whole surface once more, including over the heartgraining. Use the flogging brush to flog all the decoration just before it is dry, beating the surface with the bristles as you work down to slightly soften the markings.*

6 *Wrap the comb in a lint-free cloth. Use this tool to wipe out lines of glaze to create the lights. Flog the glaze one more time then leave to dry. Protect by applying eggshell oil varnish with a household paintbrush.*

# Pine

## Materials and Equipment

Cream oil-based eggshell paint
   for the base coat
Artist's oil paints: raw umber,
   raw sienna, white
White spirit
Paint kettles
Roller and tray
Household paintbrushes,
   fitch brush, hog-hair
   softening brush
Heartgrainer
Rubber comb
Eggshell oil varnish

This paint effect introduces a variety of processes and is a good finish to practise to acquire familiarity and confidence with specialist tools and techniques. The real wood is now easily obtainable and affordable, so you might prefer to use this method to produce fantasy versions using unconventional colours. Bear in mind, however, that you need to keep the tones of the base colour and the top glaze coat close together.

1 *Apply the base coat with a roller. Mix raw umber, raw sienna and white oil paints to replicate the colour of pine. Mix 1 part paint to 2 parts white spirit. Apply the glaze with a brush, then drag a dry brush through the glaze, working in a straight line in one direction.*

2 *To suggest planks of wood, hold the brush on its side at a slight angle so that more pressure is applied on the side closest to you. Pull down, removing glaze in the first instance and causing it to collect on the other side of the brush. Each plank should be about the width of a heartgrainer's head.*

3 *Twist a dry fitch brush into the glaze to create the knots. The more pressure you apply to the brush the wider the imprint will be. Aim for a random, natural look.*

4 *Soften the knots and the effect so far by gently wiping over the surface in different directions with a dry brush.*

5 *Pull a heartgrainer through the glaze, pivoting the rubber head. Add heartgraining to each plank, altering the angle as you rock and pivot to ensure each plank is different. Pull a rubber comb through the glaze over the heartgraining.*

6 *Soften off the decoration with a hog-hair softening brush while it is still tacky. Follow the graining first then gently wipe against the grain to give a slightly blurred effect. Leave to dry. Protect by applying eggshell oil varnish.*

# Bird's-eye maple

## Materials and Equipment

Pale off-white eggshell paint
 for the base coat
Artist's oil paints: raw sienna,
 yellow ochre, raw umber
Oil-based glaze
White spirit
Paint kettles
Household paintbrushes,
 fine artist's brush,
 hog-hair softening brush
Decorator's sponge
Eggshell oil varnish

Bird's-eye maple has a unique appearance with small eyes or dots appearing regularly in the grain. These can vary in size and form no particular pattern. This imitation wood effect is best achieved in oil glazes that dry slower than water-based varieties and so give you the time you need to manipulate the effect and achieve the maple look. Although suitable for large areas, this wood finish often looks better if worked in panels.

1 Apply the base coat with a roller. Mix raw sienna, yellow ochre, and raw umber artist's oil paints to produce a golden brown maple shade. Mix equal amounts of paint and oil-based glaze, then equal amounts of maple glaze and white spirit. Use a brush to wash on the glaze.

2 Pull a clean paintbrush down through the glaze in a regular wiggling motion to add the pattern of a loose series of bands.

3 Use a sponge to lightly dab off areas where the glaze is too wet.

4 To create the eyes, dab the glaze in places using your knuckle and fingertips.

5 Use a fine artist's brush to paint in large dots of the maple glaze mixed in Step 1, keeping the spacing random.

6 As the glaze dries to a slightly tacky finish, soften the effect by lightly brushing all over in varying directions with a hog-hair softening brush. Leave to dry, then seal with eggshell oil varnish.

# Fruitwood

## Materials and Equipment

Cream oil-based eggshell paint
  for the base coat
Artist's oil paints: burnt umber,
  burnt sienna, white
White spirit
Paint kettles
Roller and tray
Household paintbrushes,
  pointed fitch brush,
  hog-hair softening brush
Heartgrainer
Rubber comb
Lint-free cloth
Eggshell oil varnish

This effect is a fantasy finish based on an imitation of fruitwoods that were often combined when there was not enough of one wood available to complete a whole piece. It uses a variety of techniques to texture the finish and to produce the characteristic knots and graining, similar to those of many hardwoods. You could add more marking to suggest aging in the patina by adding and manipulating another thin glaze layer.

1 *Apply the base coat with a roller. Mix burnt umber, burnt sienna and white oil paints to give a red-brown wood shade. Mix 1 part paint to 2 parts white spirit. Brush on the glaze then drag the brush back through, working in a straight line in one direction.*

2 *Hold a brush at right angles to the surface. Push the bristles into the glaze until they splay out, producing a wood texture of graining and knots. Repeat all over.*

3 *Pull the brush through the glaze with its bristles splayed out to continue the texturing.*

4 *Pull a heartgrainer through the glaze, pivoting the rubber head. Add more heartgraining, leaving small, irregular gaps between each strip and altering the angle as you rock and pivot. Pull a rubber comb through the glaze, over the heartgraining.*

5 *To suggest knots and eyes, use a pointed fitch brush to apply circles of glaze. Wrap a lint-free cloth over a finger and press into the glaze eye to emphasise and highlight the shape.*

6 *Use a fitch brush to paint in more darks to suggest random eyes and knots. Soften the whole surface by brushing over in a variety of directions with a hog-hair softening brush. Leave to dry. Protect by applying eggshell oil varnish.*

# Mahogany

## Materials and Equipment

Dark pink oil-based eggshell
  paint for the base coat
Artist's oil paints: alizarin
  crimson, burnt sienna,
  burnt umber
White spirit
Paint kettles
Roller and tray
Household paintbrushes,
  hog-hair softening brush
Eggshell oil varnish

Mahogany is well known for its distinctive colouring and pronounced areas of grain. Here we demonstrate how to simulate the flame grain from the topmost part or where the branches come off the main section. It is traditional to use the flame cross-section for the inner panels of doors. The effect can be deepened with an additional burnt umber glaze applied and manipulated over the red decoration.

1 Apply the base coat with a roller. This finish should be worked in panels. Mix alizarin crimson and burnt sienna oil paints to give a mahogany red-brown shade. Mix equal amounts of paint and white spirit and brush on the glaze.

2 Mix alizarin crimson and burnt umber oil paints to make a darker, brown-red shade and dilute with an equal amount of white spirit. Loosely brush on this darker shade in the centre and at the outer edges of the panel.

3 Scrub a dry brush into the glaze in successive arcs, repeating the curve to begin suggesting the flame effect. Do not stop the movement of the brush but try to complete each arch continuously.

4 Soften off the whole surface with gentle strokes of a hog-hair softening brush, working against the grain to slightly blur the lines.

5 Pull a dry brush through the glaze at the edges of the panel to suggest the straight grain that would be apparent on either side of the arc grain.

6 Use the glaze mixed in Step 2 to paint darks back into the centre where the effect may have lightened due to the arc graining motion. Soften off the whole surface and leave to dry. Protect by applying eggshell oil varnish with a household paintbrush.

# Peeling paint

## Materials and Equipment

Coarse-, medium-, and fine-
    grade wet-dry sandpapers
Wire brush
Matt emulsion paints: red,
    blue, pale blue
Water-based crackle medium
Household paintbrushes
Hair dryer or hot-air gun
Dead flat acrylic varnish

Crackle medium used between two layers of paint produces a random distressed effect, as if the paint has peeled back naturally after exposure to the elements. The water-based medium causes the top layer of colour to become brittle and crack, leaving a patterned surface. The medium can be reactivated with water, so a third, watery colour is easily lifted off. For maximum effect use contrasting colours.

1 *Sand the surface to remove any varnish or paint then wire brush the wood to bring out the grain and provide a key. Brush on a coat of red matt emulsion paint, making sure the surface is well covered. Leave to thoroughly dry.*

2 *Brush on a layer of water-based crackle medium, working quickly and evenly and following the manufacturer's instructions. Leave to dry.*

3 *Apply a top coat of blue matt emulsion paint using quick brushstrokes. Do not work back over the paint but use single strokes to cover in one attempt – the crackle medium is activated immediately and will lift off the top coat if disturbed.*

4 *Warm up the top coat with a hair dryer or a hot-air gun. Do not hold the heat source too close or the paint will bubble. As the paint dries it will crack, revealing the base colour. Leave to dry completely.*

5 *Wash over with a watery mix of pale blue matt emulsion paint using quick brushstrokes. This watery mix will reactivate the crackle medium, making it possible to move the top coat.*

6 *Gently push the side of the brush into the pale blue top coat. This will lift up some paint without smudging. Continue lifting off areas to suggest peeling. When satisfied, leave to dry. Seal with dead flat acrylic varnish.*

# Antiquing with coloured waxes

## Materials and Equipment

Coarse-, medium-, and fine-
grade wet-dry sandpapers
Wire brush
Methylated spirits
Lint-free cloth
Fine wire wool
Waxes: cherry red, antiquing,
liming
White spirit
Clear finishing oil

This is a method similar to that traditionally used by French polishers to change the colour of wood. Thin layers of wax colour the wood without obscuring the grain. Repeated coats seal and protect the porous wood, and each layer is polished to give a fine, clear sheen that is water resistant. The friction caused by polishing heats up and softens the wax, causing it to penetrate further, resulting in a wonderful, deep patina.

1 Sand the surface to remove any varnish or paint, then wire brush the wood to bring out the grain. Repeatedly clean the surface with methylated spirits and a lint-free cloth. Change the cleaning cloth regularly and continue until the cloth comes away clean when wiped over.

2 Dip fine wire wool in white spirit and then into cherry red wax. Rub the wax into the wood, following the grain.

3 Polish the surface with a lint-free cloth to remove excess wax and give a smooth, hard finish.

4 Add antiquing wax to a few areas using fine wire wool. This will darken the colour here and there and give a deeper, richer colouration. Polish again with a lint-free cloth.

5 Apply a thin layer of liming wax with fine wire wool and polish off as before.

6 Sand lightly with fine-grade wet-dry sandpaper. Use a lint-free cloth to rub on a thin coat of clear finishing oil. Leave to dry and add another layer of oil for complete coverage. Buff to a high sheen.

# Trompe l'oeil

## Materials and Equipment

Pencil, tracing paper, transfer
paper, masking tape, biro
White undercoat
Artist's oil paints: blue, yellow,
purple, white, green,
burnt umber
White spirit
Paint palette
Artist's brushes, household
paintbrush
Oil varnishes: matt, eggshell

Trompe l'oeil means to deceive the eye. The deception with this simple project is the impression that a flower has been casually dropped on a tabletop. To achieve the effect the light source must be carefully considered, since it is the painted shadow falling to one side of the object that gives the convincing three-dimensional look. Studying the shadows cast by a real object is a great aid to successfully recreating a painted version.

1 *If you are not working on a wooden surface you can apply a faux fruitwood finish (see pages 144–145). Copy the outline shape of a real flower onto a piece of tracing paper.*

2 *Place transfer paper between the sketch and the surface and lightly fix with masking tape. Redraw the design with a biro to transfer it.*

3 *Use an artist's brush to paint the whole shape in white undercoat. Leave to dry and recoat to achieve a solid coverage. Let dry.*

4 *Squeeze a little of each of the artist's oil paints onto a palette. Dilute the blue, main flower colour with a little white spirit until fluid. Use an artist's brush to wash the colour onto the petals. Let dry.*

5 *Add a wash of yellow oil paint, diluted as in Step 4, to the centre of the flower and purple washes running out from there. Add a green wash to the stem. Mix in a little white oil paint to lighten the colours if necessary. Outline the petals with a purple wash. Leave to dry.*

6 *Use a burnt umber wash to paint in a shadow on one side of the flower and stem to add depth and suggest the three-dimensional shape of the flower lying on the surface. When dry, protect the flower with a matt oil varnish and the surrounding table with an eggshell oil varnish.*

# Drag and stipple with lining

## Materials and Equipment

White eggshell paint for the
base coat
Ruler, pencil, masking tape
Artist's oil paints: raw sienna,
burnt umber, raw umber
White spirit
Paint kettles
Household paintbrushes,
flogging brush, stippling
brush, fitch brush,
long-haired sable brush
Eggshell oil varnish

Dragging is often combined with stippling when
covering large areas or working on a surface with
awkward mouldings and panels. Here it is also
combined with lining to neaten up and enhance the
basic shape of a panel. Lining often follows the shape
of the piece being painted, at the same distance from
the edge all the way round. This method lets you use
the edge of the surface to run your brush along.

1 Apply the base coat. Mix 1 part raw sienna artist's oil paint to 2 parts white spirit and paint onto the edges of the panel. Pull a flogging brush through the wet glaze in parallel lines. Let dry.

2 Brush the same glaze mix used in Step 1 onto the central area of the panel.

3 Dab the bristles of a stippling brush quickly and evenly into the wet glaze. Leave to dry.

4 Mix burnt umber and raw sienna oil paints and add white spirit until fluid. Load onto a fitch brush. Hold one side of the brush against the edge of the panel, then pull the paint in a single movement along the edge. Line each edge and let dry.

5 Measure the width of the outer line and mask with masking tape. Using the same dilute paint as in Step 4, fill in the masked band. Paint quickly and evenly so the brush drags the paint on. Leave to dry and remove the tape.

6 Mix raw sienna, raw umber and burnt umber oil paints, adding white spirit to make the paint flow. Paint a thin line with a long-haired sable brush. Paint long runs and look ahead of the brush to avoid wobbling. Rest your little finger on the surface to steady your hand. Finally, apply eggshell oil varnish.

# Fake parquet floor

**Materials and Equipment**

Cream oil-based eggshell paint
  for the base coat
Ruler, pencil, craft knife
Manila stencil card
Artist's oil paints: raw sienna,
  white, burnt umber
White spirit
Paint kettles
Roller and tray
Household paintbrushes,
  hog-hair softening brush
  (optional)
Rubber comb
Heartgrainer
Eggshell oil varnish

A painted floor is a flexible solution to a common decorating problem: it offers an individual look with potentially stunning visual impact. This is a quick and easy way to imitate an expensive wood block floor. You can work the painting in clean, crisp lines and strong colours, or alternatively aim for a faded effect with the appearance of years of wear and tear. If protected well the finish will be easy to clean and long lasting.

1 Apply the base coat with a roller. Measure the area to be painted and decide on your pattern. Cut masks of the main shapes from stencil card. These can be used as templates when marking out the pattern as well as masks at a later stage.

2 Combine raw sienna and white oil paints to make the palest wood shade. Mix 1 part paint to 2 parts white spirit. Texture the surface by applying the glaze with a loose stipple technique. Leave to dry.

3 Use raw sienna, white and burnt umber oil paints with white spirit to mix three more wood colour glazes as in Step 2. Decide which colours will go where. Use a mask made in Step 1 to cover the surrounding planks and wash the first glaze on.

4 Repeat the glazing of the first colour on a few of the other planks.

5 Pull a rubber comb through the wet glaze to suggest wood textures. Complete all of the planks in the first colour and let dry. Repeat Steps 3–5 with the remaining glaze colours.

6 Use a heartgrainer on some of the planks and leave some without combing or heartgraining. Use a hog-hair softening brush to blur the graining if it is too bold. Add more layers if desired. Protect by applying several coats of eggshell oil varnish.

# Porphyry

## Materials and Equipment

Pink eggshell paint for the base coat
Artist's oil paints: alizarin crimson, burnt sienna, burnt umber, white
White spirit
Paint kettles
Roller and tray
Household paintbrushes, hog-hair softening brush, fitch brushes
Eggshell oil varnish

Porphyry is a hard igneous rock with a granular appearance and purple-red colour. It has few or no veins but, when polished, is similar in appearance to marble. Porphyry is a relatively easy effect to produce, but it's worth experimenting with the background colour on some trial pieces before beginning the job proper. The finished effect should be smooth to touch and can be waxed to imitate the real polished rock.

1 Apply the base coat with a roller. Mix equal amounts of alizarin crimson oil paint and white spirit. Use a brush to wash the glaze over the surface.

2 Stipple with the bristles of a hog-hair softening brush to create a smooth finish. Leave to dry.

3 Mix two red glazes using alizarin crimson and burnt sienna and alizarin crimson and burnt umber with white spirit, as in Step 1. Brush the two colours on in separate patches, stippling with a hog-hair softening brush as you go.

4 Continue adding patches of the glazes. Soften the effect so that the colours blend together to make a solid coat. Leave to dry.

5 Mix a pink glaze using white and alizarin crimson oil paints and white spirit as before. Load a fitch brush with the mix then gently knock the brush against another brush to spatter the colour. Vary the size of the dots by spattering at different distances from the surface. Leave to dry.

6 Spatter the surface with the alizarin crimson and burnt umber glaze mixed in Step 3. Keep the brushes at a constant distance from the surface for a more even spatter. Leave to dry. Protect by applying eggshell oil varnish with a household paintbrush.

# Tortoiseshell

## Materials and Equipment

Cream oil-based eggshell paint
  for the base coat
Artist's oil paints: raw sienna,
  burnt sienna, burnt umber
Oil-based glazing liquid
White spirit
Paint kettles
Household paintbrushes,
  fitch brushes, hog-hair
  softening brush
Eggshell oil varnish

The pattern commonly known as 'tortoiseshell' actually describes the shell of the sea turtle, which was once polished and turned into decorative objects. The pattern is imitated using a series of diagonal strokes in a variety of widths and lengths. It is a complex and intense pattern that usually looks its best in a design made up of small sections joined together, such as a tabletop with simple inlaid shapes.

1 *Apply the base coat with a roller. Mix equal amounts of raw sienna oil paint and oil-based glazing liquid. Mix 1 part coloured glaze to 2 parts white spirit. Brush on the glaze, work until nearly dry to give an even, smooth coverage. Allow to dry.*

2 *Use a fitch brush and raw sienna oil paint to apply a series of directional patches, with space between each shape.*

3 *Add small patches of burnt sienna oil paint here and there and larger quantities of burnt umber oil paint, following the direction of the first shapes and butting up to them in some instances.*

4 *Gently pull through with a hog-hair softening brush, following the direction of the previous brushstrokes. Use occasional cross strokes to soften the brushstrokes.*

5 *Mix equal amounts of burnt umber oil paint and white spirit. Load a fitch brush with the mix then gently knock the brush against another brush to spatter the colour. Work close to the surface to achieve a fine spattering and only over some areas. Leave for a few minutes before softening.*

6 *Repeat any of the steps to increase depth if necessary. Add a few small spots of burnt umber oil paint. Leave to dry completely. Protect by applying eggshell oil varnish with a household paintbrush.*

# Lapis lazuli

## Materials and Equipment

Pale blue oil-based eggshell
  paint for the base coat
Artist's oil paints: ultramarine,
  burnt umber, white, gold
White spirit
Paint kettles
Roller and tray
Household paintbrushes,
  hog-hair softening brush,
  stippling brush, fitch brushes
Eggshell oil varnish

Lapis lazuli is a blue mineral flecked with yellow iron pyrites, or fool's gold. It is rare and very valuable, and in earlier times was ground up as a pigment, the modern equivalent of which is ultramarine. To simulate the semi-opaque mineral, the luminosity of an ultramarine glaze is given depth and solidity by the addition of burnt umber and gold speckling in drifts and clusters, before a final waxing for added lustre.

1 *Apply the base coat with a roller. Mix equal amounts of ultramarine oil paint and white spirit. Wash the glaze over the surface.*

2 *Use a hog-hair softening brush, or stippling brush if working over a large area, to stipple the blue to give an even finish. Leave to dry.*

3 *Mix burnt umber and ultramarine oil paints to achieve a darker blue and dilute with white spirit as in Step 1. Paint on separate patches of this glaze and the original ultramarine glaze.*

4 *Stipple with a stippling brush to blend the two colours on the surface. Let dry.*

5 *Add white to ultramarine oil paint to make a light blue and mix with an equal amount of white spirit. Load the glaze onto a fitch brush then gently knock the brush against another brush to spatter the colour. Work close to the surface to spatter a fine mist. Repeat to spatter the burnt umber and ultramarine glaze mixed in Step 3.*

6 *Mix equal amounts of gold oil paint and white spirit. Load a clean fitch brush with glaze. Pull back and release the bristles to spatter the surface with large dots here and there. Leave to dry. Protect by applying eggshell oil varnish with a household paintbrush.*

# Malachite

## Materials and Equipment

Turquoise oil-based eggshell
   paint for the base coat
Artist's oil paints: viridian
   green, raw umber
Oil-based glazing liquid
White spirit
Paint kettles
Household paintbrushes,
   stippling brush,
   short-bristled fitch brushes,
   hog-hair softening brush
Card
Eggshell oil varnish

Malachite is a semi-precious, bright green mineral with
a unique ornamental quality. The complex pattern of
incomplete circles and fractured bands of light and
dark green can be imitated by combing torn card
through a glaze coat to shape a series of half circles.
The uneven edges of the card imitate the random
organic pattern of the natural mineral.

1 Apply the base coat. Combine viridian green and raw umber oil paints to achieve a dark, emerald green. Mix in equal amounts with oil-based glazing liquid, then mix 1 part glaze to 2 parts white spirit.

2 Brush this mix on in an even layer. Use a stippling brush to stipple the glaze until it has an even appearance.

3 Fold a small piece of card and tear along the fold. Use the torn edge to work the glaze, pulling it through in an irregular semi-circle, leaving one corner of the card approximately in the centre. You may want to practise this action on a trial surface before beginning the decoration proper. Use new pieces of card as old ones get clogged.

4 Using the card, continue forming shapes, allowing them to overlap slightly each time. Use different sizes of card to vary the incomplete circles. In some of the gaps between combed shapes, twist a short-bristled fitch brush in the glaze to imitate the markings of the crystal patterns.

5 Load a fitch brush with more glaze and stipple in dark edges around some of the shapes. Correct any mistakes by adding more glaze and recombing. Use the end of the brush to outline each shape.

6 Soften off the patterns gently with a hog-hair softening brush, repeatedly brushing in various directions until you obtain a regular, smooth finish. Leave to dry. Protect by applying eggshell oil varnish.

# Floating marble

## Materials and Equipment

White eggshell paint for the base coat
Artist's oil paints: sap green, Payne's grey, red
Oil-based glaze
White spirit
Paint kettles
Small paintbrushes, hog-hair softening brush, fitch brush
Lint-free cloth
Ruler, pencil, masking tape, red permanent marker pen
Eggshell oil varnish

Floating marble, also known as fossil marble, can only be achieved successfully on a flat surface due to the spattered white spirit. This effect does not imitate a particular marble and so can be created in any mix of colours. It is a random finish: the colours blend when white spirit is added and the patterns produced will vary according to how much spirit is used. Marking out squares like floor tiles gives an edge to the finish.

1 Apply the base coat. Make three glazes by mixing sap green, Payne's grey, and red oil paints each with an equal amount of oil-based glaze. Mix equal amounts of each glaze and white spirit. Wash on patches of each glaze.

2 Remove some of the colour with a pad of soft, lint-free cloth until a thin coat is achieved.

3 Soften the brushstrokes and blend the colours by brushing over in a variety of directions with a hog-hair softening brush.

4 Load a fitch brush with white spirit then gently knock the brush against another brush to spatter the colour. Shake a fitch brush loaded with white spirit over the surface and dab it into the paints to vary the pattern. Leave to dry.

5 Mark the surface into squares and mask with masking tape. Mix equal amounts of Payne's grey oil paint and white spirit and use it to tint eggshell oil varnish. Varnish alternate panels with tinted varnish and the remaining with clear varnish. Let dry.

6 Remove the tape and draw over the dividing lines between each square with a red permanent marker pen.

# Metallic
## effects

Metallic finishes have come into their own since paints, powders, metal leaf and what was once specialist equipment have become widely available. Traditional gilding is a wonderful craft to master, with a little time and patience, but there are also less costly and time-consuming results to be found using imitation gold and silver leaf and transfer metal leaf. These simpler techniques will introduce beginners to the craft of gilding while also introducing a greater range of possibilities than might have been associated with the tradition. The use of bronze powders offers another gilded effect at a vastly reduced cost, the colours and techniques providing a fascinating array of decorative finishes, while combining metal leaf, metallic paints and powders allows you to produce rich and varied finishes that are completely unique.

Patination of metals was traditionally shrouded in secrecy, but this section demonstrates some easy methods of patination using readily available chemicals. It also explores methods of contrasting matt and metallic finishes to create interesting and unusual results. The most important issue with metallic work is to experiment and record the results so that you gain a thorough understanding of the accidental mixes possible and can replicate any finish.

# Metallic paints

## Materials and Equipment

Blue matt emulsion paint for
  the base coat
Metallic water-based paints:
  pale silver, copper,
  deep silver
Ultramarine acrylic paint
Paint kettles
Household paintbrushes
Fine wire wool
Beeswax or high-gloss varnish
Lint-free cloth

The shimmer of the metallic paints as they catch and reflect the light makes this a dramatic effect that offers endless possibilities for use both in and outside the home. The regularity of the mix of colours can be controlled to give a subtle, easy-on-the-eye finish to any decorative scheme.

1 Apply the base coat with a paintbrush. Lightly load a household paintbrush with pale silver metallic water-based paint and apply broken brushstrokes in a thread-like vertical layer. Keep the brushstrokes straight and short. Leave to dry.

2 Brush on cross-hatching patches of copper and deep silver metallic water-based paints. Alternate the size and colour of each patch and brush the patches of colour lightly into each other.

3 Add a little ultramarine acrylic paint to blue matt emulsion paint to create a deep blue. Using the same subtle approach as before, repeat the cross-hatching using the original blue emulsion paint and the new, deeper blue mix. Brush these lightly into the patches of metallic paint. Leave to dry.

4 Repeat Step 2 using copper and pale silver metallic paints. This softens the colours slightly and adds more depth. Keep adding layers until the desired balance of colour and texture is achieved. Allow to dry.

5 Rub over the entire surface with fine wire wool to smooth the patina and add variety to the texture.

6 The metallic paints may tarnish if the surface is left unprotected. So, apply a coat of liquid beeswax or high-gloss varnish with a paintbrush. Buff to a sheen with a lint-free cloth when dry.

# Metallic and matt paints

## Materials and Equipment

Pink matt emulsion paint for
  the base coat
Metallic water-based paints:
  copper, blue
White matt emulsion paint
Household paintbrushes
Paint kettle
High-gloss varnish or beeswax
Lint-free cloth

Metallic and matt paints can be combined over a surface and the colours blended, like a colourwash, to create a restful atmosphere. It is a good idea to practise dry-brushing because you do not want to overload the brush and obscure previously applied colours. Thinning the paints slightly with water will help the flow. The contrasting matt and metallic areas should be well mixed to give an even appearance.

1 Apply the base coat with a paintbrush. Load a brush with copper metallic water-based paint and lightly drag the paint onto the surface in one direction. Use short brushstrokes to help keep the lines straight. Leave to dry.

2 Dry-brush (see pages 54–55) blue metallic water-based paint in the opposite direction creating a cross-hatch pattern. Brush lightly, leaving the previous colours showing. Leave to dry.

3 Mix white and pink matt emulsion paints to make a light pink. Dry-brush it on in one direction in patches. Allow to dry.

4 Add short brushstrokes here and there of the original pink matt emulsion paint, particularly in areas where it may have become obscured.

5 Load the brush with a little copper and blue metallic paint and add thin, thread-like lines in the opposite direction to create another cross-hatch pattern. Leave to dry.

6 Apply a coat of liquid beeswax or high-gloss varnish with a paintbrush. Buff to a sheen with a lint-free cloth when dry.

# Gold-painted squares

## Materials and Equipment

Red matt emulsion paint for the base coat

Tape measure or ruler, pencil, craft knife, cutting mat, masking tape

Manila stencil card

Gold metallic water-based paint

Household paintbrushes

Fine-grade wet-dry sandpaper

Button polish or sanding sealer

Painted gold is less reflective than gold leaf, but offers a soft, warm glow. It can appear rich, luxurious and sophisticated, and ideally should be well lit to enhance its subtle reflective qualities. This grid pattern is similar to the effect you would achieve if using metal leaf. The surface to be decorated must be particularly smooth because any irregularities will be exaggerated by the linear brushstrokes.

1 Apply the base coat with a paintbrush. Using a pencil and ruler or tape measure, mark out a grid of 10-cm (4-in) squares.

2 Mark a 10-cm (4-in) square on a sheet of manila stencil card and cut out the stencil with a craft knife over a cutting mat, leaving a 3-cm (1¼-in) border all around. Cut out a number of stencils in the same way – you will need to change stencils regularly as paint builds up on them.

3 Line a stencil up on the grid on the wall and fix in place with a few pieces of masking tape. Load a brush with a little gold metallic water-based paint and brush over the stencil in one direction. Repeat in alternate squares over the whole surface. Leave to dry.

4 Repeat Step 3 on the remaining squares in the grid, this time brushing the paint on in the opposite direction. Allow to dry.

5 Smooth the finish by rubbing down lightly with fine-grade wet-dry sandpaper, following the direction of the brushstrokes where possible.

6 Finish with button polish or sanding sealer to protect the gold from tarnishing and scratching.

# Steel

## Materials and Equipment

Grey undercoat for the
base coat
Artist's silver metallic
oil-based paint
White spirit
Fine wire wool
Black shoe polish
Paint kettles
Household paintbrushes
Lint-free cloths

This paint effect has been devised to imitate the two-tone look of brushed steel. Thin layers of black shoe polish add depth to the brushed-on silver paint, dulling it to give a varied surface finish. Artist's oil-based paint is used to make the finish more hard-wearing, and should be allowed to dry thoroughly before waxing with wire wool. This metal finish works very well combined with blues and pale wood, or black and white.

1 Apply the base coat with a paintbrush. Brush on a solid layer of silver metallic oil-based paint as smoothly as possible. Allow to dry and apply a second coat if necessary to achieve a solid coverage. Leave to dry.

2 Mix equal amounts of grey undercoat and white spirit and brush on in one direction, letting the silver show through the thin glaze.

3 Lightly wipe over the grey glaze with a loose pad of lint-free cloth, following the direction of the brushstrokes. Leave to dry.

4 Dip a paintbrush in white spirit then load it with a small amount of the silver paint. Drag the brush over the surface in one direction to apply a thin layer of silver that does not obscure the darker colour underneath. Leave to dry.

5 Use fine wire wool to apply an even, thin layer of black shoe polish. Follow the direction of the brushstrokes to avoid scratching or marking the paint.

6 Buff up the polish with a soft cloth. Reapply and buff up thin layers of black shoe polish until the surface has a good covering of wax.

# Rusted iron

## Materials and Equipment

Grey undercoat for the
  base coat
Burnt umber acrylic paint
Metallic water-based paints:
  copper, silver
Matt acrylic glaze
Paint kettles
Decorator's sponge
Fitch brushes, household
  paintbrush
Whiting
Sieve and spoon
High-gloss varnish or beeswax
Lint-free cloth

This paint technique suggests the texture and colours that result from the corrosive effects on metal of the elements and the passage of time. Aging iron can appear to rot and has a crumbling, dusty appearance, here imitated with silver paint and whiting. The use of acrylic paints makes this a quick and easy effect to achieve. You could also introduce a wash of black before the copper for a dramatic colour difference.

1 *Apply the base coat with a paintbrush. Dip a damp sponge in burnt umber acrylic paint and use a circular motion to wash it on in patches. Use a stippling motion to dab on the paint in places for variety. Leave to dry.*

2 *Use a clean damp sponge to wash on patches of copper metallic water-based paint in patches of various sizes, overlapping the grey and burnt umber areas. Let dry.*

3 *Use a clean damp sponge to stipple on patches of silver metallic water-based paint. Wipe the sponge back into the paint to smooth out the effect here and there.*

4 *Mix burnt umber and copper glazes by combining equal amounts of paint, matt acrylic glaze and water. Load a fitch brush with the mix and gently knock it against another brush to spatter the colour. Spatter both glazes to suggest age spots.*

5 *Pour some whiting into a sieve and sprinkle it over the surface in patches. The whiting will adhere to the surface where wet. Leave to dry and brush off any excess if necessary.*

6 *Protect with matt acrylic glaze and high-gloss varnish or liquid beeswax applied with a paintbrush. Buff to a sheen with a lint-free cloth when dry.*

# Verdigris

## Materials and Equipment

Orange matt emulsion paint for
  the base coat
Copper metallic
  water-based paint
Aqua acrylic paint
White matt emulsion paint
Paint kettles
Household paintbrushes
Decorator's sponges
Whiting
Sieve and spoon
Fine-grade wet-dry sandpaper
Matt acrylic glaze
High-gloss varnish or beeswax
Lint-free cloth

Verdigris is a naturally occurring corrosion that can affect copper, brass and bronze. Copper verdigris is particularly attractive: the combination of the warm copper and the cool tones of the blue-green patina create an harmoniously balanced, multi-coloured finish. This painted version is easily achieved and looks authentic, and the addition of a sprinkling of whiting over the drying paint builds up the texture.

1 Apply the base coat with a paintbrush. Thoroughly sand the dry base coat with fine-grade wet-dry sandpaper to give a smooth surface.

2 Use a brush to apply a solid coat of copper metallic water-based paint, finishing the brushstrokes neatly in one direction to give an even finish. Leave to dry.

3 Use a sponge to dab on an uneven layer of aqua acrylic paint. Allow to dry.

4 Add a little white matt emulsion paint to the aqua acrylic paint to lighten it. Use a sponge to lightly dab on an uneven layer of paint, allowing the copper to show through in patches. Leave to dry.

5 Dilute each of the two shades of aqua paint with an equal amount of water. Puddle the two mixes on in patches by dipping a sponge in the dilute paint and squeezing it out over the surface. Sponge off some of the colour in places where it is too watery.

6 While the dilute paints are drying, pour some whiting into a sieve and sprinkle it over the surface. The whiting will adhere to the surface where wet. Leave to dry and brush of any excess whiting if necessary. Seal with matt acrylic glaze and a coat of liquid beeswax or high-gloss varnish applied with a paintbrush. Buff to a sheen with a lint-free cloth.

# Opalescent solid colour

## Materials and Equipment

Two-part blue opalescent
  water-based paint system
Roller and tray
Fine-grade wet-dry sandpaper
Hog-hair softening brush,
  household paintbrush
Decorator's sponge

A solid base coat and opalescent top coat can be bought as a two-part system, with colours coordinated to give the ultimate match. The final finish is a strong colour with a hint of lustre and a varied shimmer, from bright to soft depending on the build-up of layers. It is a deceptive effect that initially appears as a solid, flat colour, but as the light catches the surface you become aware of the glisten of the top coat.

1 Use a roller to apply the first layer of the blue base-coat paint of a two-part opalescent water-based paint system. Allow to dry.

2 Sand well with fine-grade wet-dry sandpaper before applying a second coat of base paint. Continue sanding and applying paint until you have a smooth, even finish with no irregularities and a solid colour coverage.

3 Dip a sponge into the second, opalescent top coat of the two-part system and wash on a smooth first coat. Leave to dry.

4 To achieve a deeper, more solid layer, use a brush to add another coat of the second, opalescent part. Working over the thin first coat will make this layer easier to brush on smoothly.

5 Before this layer has dried, brush in all directions with a hog-hair softening brush to even out the brushstrokes, blur the edges and smooth the effect. Leave to dry.

6 Use a sponge again to build up a few more thin layers of the opalescent paint, to strengthen the finish. This acrylic paint system provides a shiny, easy-to-clean surface that does not require any further protection.

# Opalescent and iridescent washes

## Materials and Equipment

White acrylic primer for the
   base coat
Tape measure, ruler, pencil
Opalescent water-based
   paints: copper, blue
Iridescent water-based paints:
   red, silver, gold
Small fitch brushes
Decorator's sponge
Fine-grade wet-dry sandpaper

Iridescent paints are lightly coloured – often appearing white on the brush – with a hint of lustre. Opalescent paints are stronger in colour with the same shimmer. Both can be built up as thin washes to produce a subtle gleam. In this instance, applying the effect over a textured wall has allowed the mixed colours to collect in the pits, while the gold wash sits on the surface – this has added depth and strengthened the colours.

1 Apply the base coat with a paintbrush. Use a tape measure, ruler and pencil to mark out a repeat diamond pattern over the surface.

2 Mix equal amounts of copper opalescent water-based paint and water. Use a sponge to wash the glaze over the large areas of a row of diamonds, and a small fitch brush to work into the edges and points. Leave to dry.

3 Combine equal amounts of blue opalescent paint and water and wash onto the adjacent rows of diamonds as before. Let dry. Add more coats if desired to make a more solid finish. Leave to dry.

4 Sand all over with fine-grade wet-dry sandpaper to blur the sharp edges of the geometric shape slightly and add interest and texture. Use a damp sponge to wash off the pencil lines if necessary.

5 Use red iridescent water-based paint over the copper and silver iridescent paint over the blue to add highlights and lowlights. Use a brush to apply the colour on the edges and points, and a sponge to pull the colour into the shape slightly and soften the brushstrokes. Leave to dry.

6 Dilute equal amounts of gold iridescent paint and water and use a sponge to wash a thin glaze all over. The gold will be quite transparent. This warm layer will soften the design a little so it is less sharply defined. These shiny acrylic paints are easy to clean and the surface does not require protection.

# Mixing lustre paints

## Materials and Equipment

Acrylic primer
Acrylic paints: pale yellow,
 deep yellow, yellow ochre
Lustre powder
Paint kettles
Household paintbrushes
Decorator's sponge

A simple, curved object can be greatly enhanced by lustre paints – the light landing on the object in varying ways will exaggerate the opalescent finish. It is easy to make your own glimmering paints using powders or clear solutions mixed with the water-based colour of your choice. Applying the colour in washes means it won't be too dominant and allows you to build up a strong, permanent finish.

1 Make sure the surface is grease free and apply six coats of acrylic primer to give a smooth surface. The absorbent, chalky finish of the primer will cover a pitted, rough surface perfectly.

2 Make opalescent paints by separately mixing equal amounts of the three shades of yellow acrylic paints and lustre powder, then, for each, combining equal amounts of paint and water. Use a brush to apply the first, pale yellow mix in a loose band at the top of the surface. Soften the brushstrokes with a sponge. Leave to dry.

3 Use a clean brush to apply a wash of the deep yellow in a loose band under the first, softening the brushmarks as before. Leave to dry.

4 Add the final, yellow ochre lustre paint wash in a band at the bottom of the surface.

5 Use a sponge to wash the lightest yellow lustre glaze all over.

6 Repeat any of the steps as necessary to deepen the colours. The shiny acrylic finish does not need further protection.

# Bronze powders

## Materials and Equipment

Grey undercoat for the
  base coat
Protective face mask
  and gloves
Pencil, tracing paper, thin card,
  transfer paper, masking
  tape, biro
Acrylic or oil gold size
Bronze powders: gold, copper
Fine sable brushes, household
  paintbrush
Fine-grade wet-dry sandpaper
High-gloss varnish or
  liquid beeswax
Lint-free cloth

Bronze powders are made from the fine powders of metals and can be found in varying shades of gold, silver and copper. Their versatility means they can be sprinkled over tacky size or mixed with a binder such as glaze, varnish, shellac or water-based paints. The powders do not produce the same shine as metal leaf but they are much easier to use and cheaper to buy. The powders are very fine and should not be inhaled.

1 *Choose simple motifs with fine points and broad areas to make good use of this method. With a pencil, draw the motifs on tracing paper, then photocopy onto thin card. Keep the images simple.*

2 *Wearing gloves, apply the base coat and sand smooth with fine-grade wet-dry sandpaper. The dusty finish of the grey undercoat will act as a contrast to the sized areas so you can view them.*

3 *Place transfer paper behind the card and tape both to the surface. Use a biro to draw around the motif and transfer it to the surface. Transfer all the motifs in the same way, keeping the overall design random with space between each image.*

4 *Use a fine sable brush to fill in the shapes with size. Make sure you have a solid layer of size since it is not possible to touch up any missed areas later without ruining the effect. Leave until tacky.*

5 *Wear a mask and pick up a little gold bronze powder on a fine sable brush. Paint it along one edge of a sized motif then feather it into the middle of the design, aiming for a shaded look that fades out towards the other edge. You do not want a solid cover. Use a sable brush to dust off excess powder.*

6 *Apply copper bronze powder, working along the opposite edge of the sized shape and feathering the powder in to meet the gold. A less covered inner area will appear darker as the grey background shows through. Seal the surface with high-gloss varnish or beeswax as protection from oxidation.*

# Water gilding with real gold

## Materials and Equipment

Heatproof bowl, mixing bowls,
  saucepan
Ready-mixed gesso
Red bole
Rabbit-skin size
Distilled water
Whiting
Scissors
Gold transfer leaf
Hog-hair brush, soft brush
Lint-free cloth
Agate burnisher

When gold leaf is applied over multiple layers of gesso and a water-based size, it can be burnished to a shiny, gleaming intensity with an agate burnisher. This also forces the metal leaf to adhere and makes it more resistant to damage. The gesso acts as a cushion for the gold when burnishing and should be smooth enough not to tear the leaf. The red bole provides colour enrichment.

1 Boil water in a saucepan. Place ready-mixed
gesso in a heatproof mixing bowl in the hot water.
Stir until melted to the consistency of single cream.
Ensure the surface is grease and dust free. Paint on
eight layers of gesso with a hog-hair brush, applying
each layer while the last is matt but still damp.

2 Smooth the surface with a small piece of wet
cloth. Prepare red bole and a rabbit-skin size and
distilled water mix (see page 19), and combine 1 part
bole with ¾ parts size. Use a clean cloth to apply a
few even, smooth coats of the mix. Leave to dry.

3 Dust a pair of scissors with whiting and cut up
small pieces of gold transfer leaf. Prepare a
rabbit-skin size and distilled water mix (as in Step 2
but without the bole dye) and brush over the surface.

4 Work quickly to apply the leaf. Dust your fingers
with whiting, then lift a small piece of leaf by the
backing paper and position it on the surface. Rub the
backing paper with a soft brush. The paper will peel
away from the leaf as the metal adheres.

5 Continue adding transfer leaf, overlapping the
pieces, to cover the surface. Tamp the gold down
with a soft brush, taking care not to tear it, and dust
off the excess leaf.

6 Leave the size to dry. Apply another layer of gold,
using less size, if necessary, to achieve a solid
coverage. Burnish the leaf with an agate burnisher.
Burnished leaf does not need extra protection.

# Oil gilding with real silver

## Materials and Equipment

Heatproof bowl, mixing bowl,
   saucepan
Ready-mixed gesso
Blue bole
Rabbit-skin size
Distilled water
Oil-based gold size
Whiting
Scissors
Silver transfer leaf
Hog-hair brush, soft brushes
Lint-free cloth
Fine wire wool
Gilding medium
   such as Ormoline

Using a quick-drying, oil-based size makes gilding small objects with transfer metal leaf a quick and easy technique. Here, thin, delicate silver leaf has been used, so repeated layers of gesso must be as smooth as possible to prevent tearing. Silver leaf from different sources can vary in colour, so make sure you purchase enough leaf for your project. The blue bole under the leaf adds interest when revealed by distressing.

1 *Pour boiling water into a heatproof bowl. Place ready-mixed gesso in a mixing bowl in the water. Stir the gesso until melted to the consistency of single cream. Ensure the surface is grease and dust free. Paint on eight layers of gesso with a hog-hair brush, applying each layer while the last is matt but damp. Polish with a wet cloth to smooth the surface.*

2 *Prepare blue bole and a rabbit-skin size and distilled water mix (see page 19), and combine 1 part bole with ¾ parts size. Use a soft brush to paint it onto the surface. Keep the bole warm and fluid over a saucepan of hot water. Leave to dry.*

3 *Ensure the surface is completely free of dust, grit or hairs. Use a soft brush to apply oil-based gold size. Make sure the surface is completely covered. Leave for the appropriate drying time, following the manufacturer's instructions.*

4 *Dust your fingers and scissors with whiting. Cut small pieces of silver transfer leaf. Lift a piece by the backing paper and position it on the surface. Rub the backing paper with a soft brush. The paper will peel away from the leaf as the metal adheres.*

5 *Continue adding transfer leaf, overlapping the pieces, to cover the surface. Use a soft brush to dust off the excess leaf. Leave the size to dry.*

6 *Distress the leaf by gently rubbing the surface with fine wire wool. Protect with gilding medium or let natural patination enhance the look.*

# Imitation gold and silver transfer leaf

## Materials and Equipment

Heatproof bowl, mixing bowl
Ready-mixed gesso
Acrylic paints: yellow, red, blue
Acrylic gold size
Whiting
Scissors
Imitation gold and silver
  transfer leaf
Household paintbrushes,
  hog-hair brush, gilder's mop
  or soft brush
Fine wire wool, fine-grade
  wet-dry sandpaper
Shellac or sanding sealer

Imitation gold – also known as Dutch metal and brass leaf – and silver leaf – also called aluminium leaf – is widely available and a cheaper alternative to the real thing. The leaf can be applied over any tacky adhesive, even household glue or varnish, but a specialist gilding size is recommended if you wish to have more control and achieve a long-lasting finish. Transfer leaf is easier to use than the loose form, although more expensive.

1 *Cover the surface with eight coats of gesso (see Step 1, page 191). Leave to dry.*

2 *Use fine wire wool and fine-grade wet-dry sandpaper to lightly rub down the surface. Touch up with gesso and repeat if necessary.*

3 *Brush on a base coat of the acrylic paints (you may need to apply two coats). Rub down the surface again with wire wool and wet-dry sandpaper. Brush on acrylic gold size to cover the surface.*

4 *Dust your hands and some sharp scissors with whiting, then cut up sheets of imitation gold and silver transfer leaf into workable pieces.*

5 *Lift a small piece of transfer leaf by the backing paper and position it on the sized surface. Rub over the backing paper with a gilder's mop or soft brush. The paper will peel away from the leaf as the metal adheres.*

6 *Continue adding transfer leaf, overlapping the pieces, to cover the surface. Dust off the excess leaf with a hog-hair or soft brush. Gently rub the surface with fine wire wool to distress it and protect with shellac or sanding sealer.*

# Copper loose leaf

## Materials and Equipment

Orange matt emulsion paint for
the base coat
Acrylic gold size
Whiting
Copper loose leaf
Firm card cut slightly larger
than a sheet of loose leaf
Household paintbrushes,
gilder's mop or soft brush
Button polish or sanding sealer
High-gloss varnish
or liquid beeswax
Lint-free cloth

Copper adds an unusual, bright, reflective quality to any scheme, and is more subtle than gold or silver. It works particularly well when combined with dark wood and warm colours such as terracotta or lilac. The easiest way to use loose metal leaf is on a flat surface, as demonstrated here. Make sure you work away from any gusts of wind because the leaf is extremely light.

1 *Apply the base coat. Brush on an even coat of acrylic gold size. Work quickly and in manageable-sized sections because the size dries fast.*

2 *Cover your fingers and a piece of firm card with whiting to stop the leaf sticking. Waft the card at the edge of the leaf book until the top sheet lifts up. Slip the card under and lift the sheet. Hold the card at an angle to the surface and touch the size with one side of the leaf. Pull the card down and away quickly, lowering the rest of the leaf.*

3 *Follow Steps 1–2 to apply adjacent sheets of copper leaf, overlapping the edges. Use the card as a straight edge to carefully tear away the excess leaf on the overlapped edges. Remember to dust your fingers and the card with whiting regularly.*

4 *Remove smaller pieces of loose leaf by gently brushing over the squares with a gilder's mop or a soft brush. This action will also press the leaf down more firmly onto the tacky size. Keep the excess leaf pieces for future use.*

5 *Seal the surface with button polish or sanding sealer to protect the leaf from tarnishing and give a hard finish to protect against scratches.*

6 *Apply high-gloss varnish or liquid beeswax with a paintbrush and buff it up to a soft sheen with a lint-free cloth.*

# Gilding on glass

## Materials and Equipment

Pane of glass
Glass cleaner, lint-free cloth
Gelatin capsule
Distilled water
Mixing bowl, heatproof bowl
Whiting
Silver loose leaf
Firm card cut slightly larger
  than a sheet of loose leaf
Household paintbrushes,
  gilder's mop or soft brush
Blackboard paint

This is a simple version of an 18th-century gilding technique that is still in use today. Silver leaf is applied to the reverse of a sheet of glass and sealed with paint, usually black. The gilding is seen through the glass, which becomes a kind of mirror, although the reflections are soft. You may want to practise the technique with imitation silver loose leaf before using the more expensive and lighter, real silver leaf.

1 Clean both sides of the glass thoroughly. Lay the glass on a dust-free surface with a block under one edge to raise the pane at an angle so that excess size can run down. Prepare to start at the raised edge and place a book of silver loose leaf nearby.

2 Take half a gelatin capsule and 300ml (½ pint) of distilled water. Warm a little water and add to the capsule to dissolve it. Top up with the rest of the cold water and stir. Brush the size onto the glass in manageable-sized sections.

3 Cover the glass with a layer of silver loose leaf (see Steps 2–4, page 197). When the glass is completely covered, leave to dry.

4 Hold the glass panel over steam for a few seconds to allow the size to cure. This will help the leaf to settle and smooth out any wrinkles. Double gild if required, using less size. Steam again.

5 Use a soft brush or a gilder's mop to gently brush off the excess loose leaf. Don't worry if the leaf has not adhered in places; these gaps will reveal the background paint and add character to the effect. Brush the excess into a container to save it.

6 Ensure the surface is free of particles, then paint on the background colour. This is traditionally black. Blackboard paint is quick drying and will protect the silver from tarnishing. Leave to dry.

# Metallic paint and metal leaf

## Materials and Equipment

Grey matt emulsion paint for
  the base coat
Tape measure, ruler, pencil,
  craft knife, cutting mat,
  masking tape
Manila stencil card
Silver metallic water-based
  paint
Acrylic gold size
Imitation silver loose leaf
Household paintbrushes,
  small brush
High-gloss varnish
  or liquid beeswax
Soft, lint-free cloth

A simple square pattern is made more interesting by combining hard with soft and light with dark, with a hard, bright, imitation silver leaf highlighting the softer, silver metallic paint. When used for wall decoration this effect will be greatly affected by the light sources. Direct light will reflect off the bright metal leaf, softer light will give it all a soft shimmer.

1 Apply the base coat with a paintbrush. Mark out a grid of squares of your preferred size. Keep the squares equal.

2 Use a craft knife to cut out a square stencil to match the size of the squares on the wall, leaving a 3-cm (1¼-in) border all around. Keep the cut-out square and find the centre point. Cut a smaller square into this stencil. Cut out a number of stencils in the same way – you will need to change them regularly as paint builds up.

3 Drag a light layer of silver metallic water-based paint all over the surface, keeping the lines parallel. Leave to dry.

4 Line the first stencil up on the grid and fix in place with masking tape. Stipple the silver metallic paint through the stencil and repeat in alternate squares over the whole surface. Let dry.

5 Use the second stencil to mark a small square in the centre of the alternate, unstencilled squares. Use a small brush to fill in the area with acrylic gold size. Leave until tacky.

6 Lay imitation silver loose leaf over the size to cover it (see Steps 4–6, page 197). Brush off excess leaf with a soft brush. Protect with high-gloss varnish or liquid beeswax. Buff with a lint-free cloth.

# Oil and water on metal leaf

## Materials and Equipment

Acrylic gold size
Whiting
Imitation silver transfer leaf
Crimson acrylic paint
Payne's grey artist's oil paint
White spirit
Paint kettles
Fitch brush, household
  paintbrush, gilder's mop or
  soft brush, hog-hair brush
Decorator's sponge
Eggshell artist's oil varnish
High-gloss varnish or
  liquid beeswax
Lint-free cloth

This subtle finish relies on a variable light source to demonstrate the full effect. The first acrylic paint washed over the metal leaf will not be lifted by the white spirit that is used to paint circles into grey artist's oil paint. The hand-drawn quality of the painted circles is in contrast with the smooth, even finish of the leaf. Try to keep the brushstrokes quick and light to achieve a spontaneous effect.

1 Cover the surface with a layer of imitation silver transfer leaf (see Steps 4–6, page 195). Mix equal amounts of crimson acrylic paint and water and wash it over the silver with a sponge. Leave to dry.

2 Combine equal amounts of Payne's grey oil paint and white spirit and use a clean sponge to wash the glaze all over. Wipe lightly to avoid disturbing the leaf

3 While the oil paint is still drying, dip a fitch brush in white spirit and paint repeated circles a regular distance apart. This will remove some of the oil paint but not the crimson acrylic wash.

4 Dab a sponge over the circles to lift off more of the paint.

5 When the paint is still tacky, lightly soften by brushing in all directions with a hog-hair softening brush. Leave to dry.

6 Seal with eggshell oil varnish followed by high-gloss varnish or liquid beeswax applied with a paintbrush. Finally, buff with a lint-free cloth.

# Metallic paint patination

## Materials and Equipment

Red matt emulsion paint for the base coat
Acrylic gold size
Whiting, scissors
Imitation gold transfer leaf
Metallic water-based paints:
  pale green, bright green, gold, copper
Paint kettles
Decorator's sponge
Household paintbrushes, gilder's mop or soft brush
Fine wire wool
Lint-free cloth
High-gloss varnish or liquid beeswax

The interplay of metallic paint and the brilliant shine of metal leaf produces a wealth of interesting layered textures. The metallic paints look like a matt wash in contrast with the extreme bright shine of the imitation gold leaf, while a wax finish adds a unified, soft glow to the effect. The background of metal leaf gives an overall impression of solidity and permanence that is not possible with just paint.

1 Apply the base coat. Cover with a layer of imitation gold transfer leaf (see Steps 4–6, page 195). Mix equal amounts of pale green metallic water-based paint and water. Use a sponge to wash the mix over the whole surface. Leave to dry.

2 Add a light textured effect by stippling on areas of bright green metallic paint, using the sponge, then wiping it back as it starts to dry. Leave to dry.

3 Stipple on the bright green metallic paint in areas once again. The build-up of layers will add depth. Leave to dry.

4 Dilute bright green, gold and copper metallic water-based paints by mixing 1 part paint to 2 parts water. Load a brush with the first colour and pull back and release the bristles to spatter the surface. Repeat with the other dilute paints.

5 Use the sponge to remove excess water and to add texture – the spattered watery paints will lift some of the washes of colour. Sponge lightly so you do not remove all the colour. Leave to dry.

6 Use a lint-free cloth and some fine wire wool to rub off patches of paint here and there. This will remove some of the thin metal and expose the red base colour. Protect with high-gloss varnish or liquid beeswax applied with a paintbrush, and then buff.

# Distressing with spirit dyes

## Materials and Equipment

Yellow matt emulsion paint for the base coat
Acrylic gold size
Whiting
Imitation silver transfer leaf
Spirit dyes: yellow, sepia, brown, red, green
Methylated spirits
Paint kettles
Household paintbrushes, hog-hair softening brush, fitch brushes
Lint-free cloth
Fine wire wool
Button polish or sanding sealer

Spirit dyes can be applied to metal leaf to achieve a controlled distressed finish, imitating the age spots and tarnishing that occur with time. The dyes will bleed into each other and have a transparency that allows the gleam of the metallic base to show through. Using a selection of spirit dyes, you can patinate the metal to imitate the effect of chemical or natural corrosion.

1 Apply the base coat. Brush on acrylic gold size in a manageable-sized section. Leave until tacky.

2 Cover your hands with whiting. Lift a sheet of imitation silver transfer leaf by the backing paper. Hold the square as straight as possible and gently place one edge on the size with the rest of the sheet held at a 45-degree angle.

3 Swiftly lay the rest of the leaf down. Gently rub the backing paper with your fingers until the leaf adheres, then remove the paper. Continue laying the leaf, overlapping the edges slightly.

4 Use a softening brush to brush off the excess leaf and keep it in a small container. Reapply a little size to any gaps where the leaf has not adhered and use a small brush to touch up with the excess leaf.

5 Load a spirit dye on a fitch brush and pull back and release the bristles to spatter the surface. Spatter the surface lightly and build up the colours as you gain confidence. If any areas have been spattered too heavily, lift the colour off with a soft cloth soaked in methylated spirits.

6 Dip fine wire wool in methylated spirits and gently rub the surface here and there to give a slightly worn appearance. Seal the surface with button polish or sanding sealer to prevent tarnishing.

# Chemical patination

## Materials and Equipment

Various matt emulsion paints
  for the base coats
Protective face mask
  and gloves
Acrylic and oil-based gold size
Metal leaf: a selection of
  metals, loose or transfer
Metal powders: such as
  bronze, brass, and copper
Patinating fluids: such as
  copper sulphate, ammonia,
  bleach, and nitric acid
Paint kettles
Household paintbrushes,
  gilder's mop or soft brush
Button polish or sanding sealer

There is a great range of rich colour patinas that can be achieved using chemicals on metal coatings. Chemicals used include bleach, copper sulphate, ammonia and nitric acid. They can be used in combination, diluted with water and applied in multiple layers. Take great care when using chemicals, remembering to protect yourself and your surroundings.

1 Apply the base coats to wooden boards. Warm colours are best combined with real or imitation gold, copper and bronze. Black, blues and greys are suited to real and imitation silver, iron and steel.

2 Brush an even coat of acrylic gold size onto the first board.

3 Cover the board with metal leaf – loose (see Steps 1–4, page 197) or transfer (see Steps 4–6, page 195), real or imitation gold or silver, copper, or bronze. Repeat Steps 2–3 for each board. Make a note on the back of each board to help you record the effects of different chemicals on different metals.

4 Wearing gloves and a face mask and working in a well-ventilated area, experiment by brushing on the chemicals. Follow the manufacturer's instructions to dilute the chemicals for varying effects. Use a damp sponge to wash off the chemicals when the desired level of patination is achieved.

5 To try the full range of patination possibilities it is advisable to experiment with metal powders. Brush on the ready-made variety or sprinkle the powder over tacky oil-based size – this will dry thoroughly, unlike acrylic size.

6 Brush on and remove the chemicals as in Step 4. Leave the chemicals for varying lengths of time to assess different rates of colouration. Protect with button polish or sanding sealer.

# Patterns
## and motifs

An endless amount of patterned finishes can be produced using stencils, stamps and free-hand painting. Some of the techniques follow traditional guidelines while others use methods that appear simple but result in sophisticated and glamorous effects. The best results, however, almost always occur when the patterns or motifs are kept simple and clear. The interest comes from the use of transparent layers of colour, varying textures or contrasting surface finishes.

Patterns and motifs used in decoration have a variety of purposes. They are often simply devices used to introduce colour, but may also be used to add personal imagery, historical reference and visually exciting and alternative detail. Figurative elements can be seen as restrictive, but you do not have to be trapped into attempting to emulate a particular era or look. Usually the most successful adventures into this area are the simplest design classics that can be adapted to suit the mood or look of the time, such as spirals, squares and stripes. Other more personal choices will occur as experience leads you to find your own language and style. Generally, the dictate that it has all been done before should inspire rather than inhibit you as you discover that there is a wealth of successful ideas, combinations and reference to view and learn from.

# Irregular patterning

## Materials and Equipment

Stucco equipment (see page 106)
Tracing paper, pencil, transfer paper, craft knife, cutting mat, masking tape
Medium- and fine-grade sandpaper
Manila stencil card
Red oxide acrylic paint
Pale gold bronze powder
PVA or white glue
Paint kettles
Fitch brush, stencil brush
Beeswax
Lint-free cloth

Individual motifs can be stencilled over a surface in a random pattern that can simply be judged by eye. The red oxide is stencilled first to suggest the red bole used in traditional gilding. Misregistering a second stencil of gold paint gives each motif a bold appearance with a deep outline. These letter stencils have been copied from old script and could be made into words or sentences, with a bit of careful measuring and marking.

1 Apply the stucco (see pages 106–107) and use a filling knife and medium- and fine-grade sandpaper to polish the surface until the plaster has a soft sheen and is smooth to the touch.

2 Trace a motif. Place a sheet of transfer paper between the tracing paper and a sheet of manila stencil card and redraw the motif to transfer the design. Repeat with more motifs, spacing them roughly evenly in rows.

3 Use a craft knife over a cutting mat to carefully cut out the motifs. Cut out the rows of motifs to make smaller stencils.

4 Lightly fix a stencil in position with masking tape. Dip the pointed tip of a fitch brush into red oxide acrylic paint and dab off the excess paint. Stipple the paint through the stencil of one motif. Repeat to stencil motifs randomly all over. Let dry.

5 Mix 4 parts gold powder to 1 part PVA or white glue and add water a little at a time to make a paint the consistency of single cream. So that you do not end up with too much paint, add the glue to the powder and then add the water.

6 Reposition the stencil over its dry, red print, aligning it slightly off register. Dip a stencil brush in gold paint and dab off the excess. Stipple the gold paint through the stencil. Repeat for each print. Leave to dry and seal using a cloth and beeswax.

# Regular patterning

## Materials and Equipment

Acrylic primer for the base coat
Ruler, pencil, graph paper,
   transfer paper, craft knife,
   cutting mat, masking tape
Manila stencil card
Opalescent and iridescent
   water-based paints (see
   pages 184–185): such as
   gold, blue, red, orange,
   green, copper, silver, yellow
Paint palette
Small paintbrushes
Decorator's sponge
Foam roller head
Fine-grade wet-dry sandpaper

These boards have been individually painted and stencilled using some of the vast array of iridescent and opalescent water-based paints currently available. Here, lighter background colours are contrasted with stronger stencilled shapes that give a bright reflection. The stencils are hand-made and can be cut to suit the specific dimensions of any tongue-and-groove boarding.

1 Prime a wooden surface and sand smooth with fine-grade wet-dry sandpaper so that some of the grain shows through. Measure and mark equal-sized vertical strips. (Here we are using tongue-and-groove.)

2 Use a paintbrush to apply strips of opalescent and iridescent water-based paints. Here, each tongue-and-groove panel is painted a different colour. Let dry.

3 Add a second layer of colour to each strip or board to make a more solid covering. Wipe over the damp paint with a sponge to ensure no brushstrokes are visible. Leave to dry.

4 Using the measurements taken in Step 1, mark a series of geometric repeat designs on graph paper. Place transfer paper between the graph paper and manila stencil card and redraw the shapes to transfer the design. Use a craft knife over a cutting mat to cut out three different stencils.

5 Lightly fix a stencil in position with masking tape. Dip the end of a foam roller head in one of the opalescent or iridescent paints and dab off the excess. Stipple the colour through the stencil. Repeat on alternate or adjacent strips or boards. Let dry.

6 You can apply a second coat of stencilled colour for interest by aligning the stencil in a different position and using a brush for variety. These acrylic paints do not need further protection.

# Building up colours

## Materials and Equipment

Pale blue matt emulsion paint
  for the base coat
Sunflower two-part stencil
Ruler, pencil, masking tape
Matt emulsion paints: cream,
  mid-blue
Acrylic paints: green, yellow,
  yellow ochre, burnt umber
Paint kettles
Household paintbrushes
Foam roller head
Decorator's sponge
Fine-grade wet-dry sandpaper
Matt acrylic glaze

Building up layers of colour over a simple flower stencil can produce a subtle shading effect with a feeling of depth. The paint is applied lightly and overlaid carefully so that previous colours remain visible. Different tools also help to make the shading more varied, such as a foam roller head for large areas and small pieces of sponge for the shading, which also adds variety of texture. Sanding lightly softens the final effect.

1 Apply the base coat. Decide on the position of the stencil and mark a border line that will contain the stencilled design.

2 Lightly fix the stencil in place with masking tape. Dip the end of a foam roller head in cream matt emulsion paint and dab off the excess. Stipple the paint through the stencil to define the image and provide a light base to add further colours to. Leave to dry.

3 Mask the stencil against the line marked in Step 1. Mix 1 part mid-blue matt emulsion paint to 2 parts water. Brush a blue wash over the area not being stencilled. Let dry and remove the tape.

4 Use a clean roller head and yellow acrylic paint to stencil the flowers. Aim for a fairly solid layer of colour, but let the texture of the foam allow the cream to show through in places. Leave to dry.

5 Use the same technique to stencil green acrylic paint over the stems.

6 Use small pieces of sponge to stipple the edges to suggest light and shade. Use yellow ochre and a mix of yellow ochre and burnt umber on the flowers and a green and burnt umber mix on the stems. Leave to dry. Lightly sand with fine-grade wet-dry sandpaper and protect with matt acrylic glaze.

# Making a large repeat stencil

## Materials and Equipment

Tracing paper, pencil, lining
  paper, transfer paper, craft
  knife, large cutting mat,
  masking tape, ruler
Large sheets of manila
  stencil card

Large-scale ready-made stencils are expensive to buy, so it can be a good idea to make your own. It is not necessary to create multi-layered designs to arrive at an individual and appropriate decoration; repeated simple shapes can give a satisfying result. This simple repeat design could be made more elaborate with the addition of extra stencilled details, such as a shadow line or a small, separate stencilled motif.

**1** *Choose a repeat motif and simplify it, reducing it to a basic shape that will be easy to stencil and still look effective. For example, this classic border can be reduced to a single stencil featuring a double swirl. Sketch the simplified motif at a manageable size (or trace it from the original). Measure the area to be decorated and decide on the size of the stencil.*

**2** *Draw a simple measured grid over the motif, say 10 squares. Cut lining paper to the size you want the stencil to be and fill with an enlarged 10-square grid. Sketch in the enlarged design with a pencil, referring to the grid on the original sketch. When it appears to be in proportion, pencil a darker line around the design.*

**3** *Position transfer paper between the motif and a large sheet of manila stencil card and fix with masking tape. Redraw the lines to transfer the design. Use several pieces of transfer paper if the size you require is not available. Leave a 5-cm (2-inch) margin top and bottom.*

**4** *Cut out the stencil using a sharp craft knife over a large cutting mat. Keep the cutting line smooth and clean by following each curve in a flowing, steady line rather than making many small cuts. Move around the table if necessary.*

**5** *Remove the cut-out and go back over the lines, trimming away any catches that will cause the paint to bleed.*

**6** *Decide how close you want each motif to repeat and mark a straight line on each edge of the stencil. Trim the stencil to give an even border.*

# Simple mural

## Materials and Equipment

Cream matt emulsion paint for
the base coat
Tracing paper, pencil, transfer
paper, craft knife, cutting
mat, masking tape
Manila stencil card
Acrylic paints: such as yellow,
green, brown, dark purple
Paint kettles
Small paintbrushes,
stencil brush
Fine-grade wet-dry sandpaper
Matt acrylic glaze

A simple landscape mural can be painted using tracing
paper and a few stencilled details. The main areas are
blocked out in flat colour, a few of the basic details are
freehand painted, and the intricate shapes are
stencilled in flat colours to match the overall painting
style. Through careful use of closely toned colours it
has been possible to suggest the light source and
distance without adding extra shading and toning.

1 Source images and trace them at the same size or photocopy them to enlarge or reduce them. Cut stencils of the fine details, any repeats, and the shapes you do not feel confident of painting freehand (see Steps 2–3, page 213). Apply the base coat.

2 Sketch two actual-size murals onto tracing paper, the first featuring the large, solid colour areas, the second describing the slightly smaller details. Rub a soft pencil over the lines on the reverse of the paper. Position the paper the right way round on the surface and redraw over the lines to transfer the design.

3 Mix acrylic paints to achieve the desired shades. Use a small brush to paint in the main, solid colours, working neatly up to the lines. Leave to dry.

4 Position transfer paper between the second sheet of tracing paper and the painted surface and draw over the lines to transfer the design. Use a small brush to paint in the details and let dry.

5 Position the detail stencils and lightly fix with masking tape. Use a stencil brush to wipe the paint through. Let dry.

6 Lightly sand the whole surface with fine-grade wet-dry sandpaper and protect the finish with matt acrylic glaze.

# Printing blocks

## Materials and Equipment

Ruler, pencil, craft knife,
cutting mat, masking tape
Stencil acetate
Matt emulsion paints: such as
dull green, brown, purple,
grey-blue, pink
Metallic water-based paints:
such as copper, gold, silver,
bronze, green
Wooden printing blocks
Decorator's sponges

These printing blocks are made of wood with a carved, raised design. They are usually used on fabric or paper, but applying the colour to the block with a sponge allows a greater amount of paint to reach the design and it is therefore possible to print onto a harder surface such as wood or plaster. It is difficult to repeat print in the same position, so if the first print is not complete it is better to clean it off and try again.

1 Mark out the surface to be decorated with a grid of equal-sized squares.

2 Mark out and cut a stencil with the same dimensions as the squares from stencil acetate, using a sharp craft knife over a cutting mat. Reserve the cut-out square for use later.

3 Lightly fix the stencil to the surface with masking tape, lining it up with a grid square. Dip a sponge in matt emulsion paint and dab off the excess paint. Stipple the paint through the stencil. Stencil alternate squares in a regular pattern of different colours. Allow to dry.

4 Stencil the remaining squares to create a regular, equal mix of colours. Leave to dry.

5 Find the centre point of the cut-out square reserved in Step 2 and make a hole big enough to make a pencil mark through. Use this device to mark the centre point of each square on the surface.

6 Load a sponge with metallic water-based paint and press a printing block into it to pick up the colour. Press the block down firmly and evenly over the central mark. Repeat with different blocks and different colours of metallic paint.

# Vegetable stamps

## Materials and Equipment

Grey matt emulsion paint for the base coat
Masking tape, permanent marker pen, craft knife
Sharp kitchen knife
Potatoes and swedes
Matt emulsion paints: red, blue, white
Household paintbrushes
Decorator's sponges
Matt acrylic varnish

Vegetable prints can look as sophisticated and professional as any commercially available foam or block prints, if used with a sense of style and ambition. The surface offered by potatoes and swedes is very receptive to paint and relatively easy to cut. Any designs must be cut and printed quickly because when the vegetable loses its moisture the stamps will become unworkable.

1 Apply the base coat. Measure and use masking tape to mark out an inner panel on the area to be printed. Brush a solid coat of white matt emulsion paint into the panel. Leave to dry.

2 Use a sharp kitchen knife to cut potatoes and swedes neatly in half. Choose dense, hard vegetables.

3 Use a marker pen to draw out simple, graphic designs on the inside of each vegetable half. Use a sharp craft knife to cut away the background, leaving a raised motif for printing.

4 Dampen some sponges and use a brush to load the surface of each one with a different shade of matt emulsion paint. These will be used as pads to apply the paint to the vegetable stamps.

5 Press a vegetable stamp onto a paint-pad sponge, then press the stamp onto the surface to print the motif. Press down quickly and evenly, not too hard or the paint might squeeze out unevenly.

6 Repeat with the different stamps and paint colours to create a simple, bold pattern. When dry, protect by applying matt acrylic varnish with a paintbrush.

# Found-material printing

## Materials and Equipment

Cream matt emulsion paint for the base coat

Found materials such as hessian, bubble wrap, corrugated card, corks, string, carpet

Stiff card, scissors, paper, sponge

Contact adhesive, PVA or white glue

Taupe matt emulsion paint

Metallic water-based paints: copper, gold

Household paintbrushes

Foam roller

Matt acrylic varnish

Making printing blocks is one way of recycling common packaging materials such as corrugated card, bubble wrap and string. There is an element of surprise and a random nature to this method of printing, so, to eliminate the possibility of disappointment, it is recommended that you experiment with the printing on spare paper first and don't waste your time trying to use objects that do not print well.

1 Use sharp scissors to cut out rectangles of hessian and bubble wrap to create background textures. Gather a selection of textured materials, such as corks, string, copper wire and natural sponge.

2 Cut out base plates of firm card and use contact adhesive to fix your chosen articles to the card in the desired pattern. Coat the whole printing block with PVA or white glue so that it will last for more than one print. Make more printing blocks as required.

3 Experiment with each printing block on spare paper to decide which to use where. Apply matt emulsion paint to the stamp with a foam roller and press the block onto the paper to impart the print. Wipe the stamp clean with a damp sponge after printing.

4 Apply the base coat. Begin to mark out the design by printing the background textures. Roll matt emulsion paint onto the hessian and bubble wrap and press these onto the surface. Leave to dry.

5 Use bright copper metallic water-based paint to print the details over the background textures. Leave to dry.

6 Use gold metallic paint to print the final details. When dry, protect by applying matt acrylic varnish with a household paintbrush.

# Frottage

## Materials and Equipment

Maroon gloss water-based
    paint for the base coat
Purple matt emulsion paint
Matt acrylic glaze
Paint kettles
Household paintbrushes
Newsprint
Fine-grade wet-dry sandpaper
Matt acrylic varnish

The frottage technique involves rubbing newsprint over a wet glaze so that it removes some of the paint and causes the remaining colour to collect and repeat the folds and lines of the absorbent paper, resulting in irregular, loose marking and texturing that is extremely random. Keep the base and top coats very close in tone for a delicate look.

1 *The surface to be decorated must be shiny, so apply a base coat of maroon gloss water-based paint. Sand the final dry coat well with fine-grade wet-dry sandpaper.*

2 *Mix equal amounts of purple matt emulsion paint and matt acrylic glaze. Combine 1 part purple glaze to 3 parts water to make up a runny mix. Use a brush to wash this mix over the surface.*

3 *While the glaze is still wet, lay sheets of newsprint over the surface and rub the back until the paper is touching all over. Quickly pull the paper off again. This will remove some glaze and leave random marks. Leave to dry.*

4 *Wash on another coat of purple glaze. If this reactivates the glaze, then it has not been allowed to dry enough and must be cleaned off and left to dry before starting again.*

5 *Repeat Step 3 to press down and remove another layer of newsprint. Allow to dry.*

6 *Protect by applying matt acrylic varnish with a household paintbrush. The varnish will also make the top layers more transparent.*

# Sprayed leaves and cut-outs

## Materials and Equipment

Cream matt emulsion paint for
  the base coat
Craft knife
Stencil cut-outs (see pages
  212–213)
Dried leaves
Protective face mask
  and gloves
Spray adhesive
Acrylic spray paints:
  copper, bronze
Paper

This decoration has been created by spraying paint over an arrangement of dried leaves of varying sizes and the cut-out shapes and letters left over from making your own stencils. The design is informal and random. A unique and delicate shading and layering occurs when the objects are moved and then resprayed, and a variety of effects can be achieved by this method.

1 Keep the cut-outs left over from cutting your own stencils to provide you with some interesting shapes to act as masks for the spray paint.

2 Apply the base coat. Dry a selection of leaves by placing them between clean paper then newsprint in a flower press or under heavy books. Arrange the leaves on the surface.

3 When you are happy with the design, transfer each element, reverse side up, to an identical position on a sheet of paper. Wearing a mask and gloves and working in a well-ventilated area, lightly spray over the whole surface with spray adhesive.

4 Reposition the objects, glue-side down on the surface. Press down well to ensure each element is firmly attached.

5 Lightly spray the surface with copper acrylic spray paint, following the manufacturer's instructions. After about 10 minutes, lift up a couple of pieces to check whether the spray colour is deep enough. Respray to build up depth if necessary. Leave to dry.

6 Remove some or all of the motifs by picking up each corner with a craft knife. Reposition the elements so that they overlap the first prints in places. Spray with bronze acrylic spray paint. Repeat Steps 5–6 until the desired effect is achieved.

# Lining-paper bands

## Materials and Equipment

Cream matt emulsion paint for the base coat
Tape measure, ruler, pencil, scissors
Thick lining paper
Gold metallic water-based paint
Acrylic paints: red, burnt umber
Paint kettles
Household paintbrushes
Decorator's sponge
Wallpaper paste
PVA or white glue

This project demonstrates the flexibility of everyday lining paper and uses it in an alternative and dramatic way. Strips of lining paper are painted then glued to the surface as wallpaper. Cutting the paper into varyingly measured strips offers you flexibility when decorating, allowing you to rearrange the colour and pattern combinations as you wish.

1 Apply the base coat. Mark a horizontal line where you want the lining paper bands to start, then mark a few more lines to act as guides later on.

2 Measure and mark up lengths of lining paper into bands of varying widths. Mark extra on the length to allow for any mistakes. Cut out the strips.

3 Use a brush to paint some of the strips with solid gold metallic water-based paint and red and burnt umber acrylic paints. Leave to dry.

4 Dilute red and burnt umber paints each with equal amounts of water. Use a damp sponge to wash these dilute paints onto the remaining lining paper strips. These colours will be more muted and may need more than one layer applied. Leave to dry.

5 On a separate surface, arrange the strips until you find the desired colour and pattern combinations. Overlap the bands if desired and aim to leave strips of the base coat showing through occasionally.

6 Glue down the bands, starting at the first line marked in Step 1. Use wallpaper paste on the wider pieces and PVA or white glue for the finer strips. As you position the paper bands, wipe over each one with a damp sponge to help press the paper down and clean off any excess glue.

# Circles

## Materials and Equipment

Grey matt emulsion paint for
 the base coat
Container lids, pencil
Metallic water-based paints:
 silver, gold, copper
Household paintbrushes,
 fitch brush, artist's brush
Damp cloth
Fine-grade wet-dry sandpaper
Satin acrylic varnish

No special drawing or measuring skills are required to
paint these bold circles since each shape is simply
created by drawing around a circular household object,
such as a container lid, and each circle is placed by
eye. Use a quality brush to paint in the circles and use
fluid brushstrokes, following the shapes carefully to
avoid going over the outline.

1 Apply the base coat. Sand the final dry coat well with fine-grade wet-dry sandpaper.

2 Brush on a solid coat of silver metallic water-based paint as evenly as possible. Leave to dry.

3 Lightly sand the silver with fine-grade wet-dry sandpaper to add texture.

4 Select two circular household objects, one larger than the other. Use a pencil to draw around the larger circle. Repeat all over the surface, aiming to retain a regular-sized gap between each circle. Position the smaller circular object centrally, by eye, in the larger circle and draw around it as before.

5 Use a fitch brush to paint the inner circles with gold metallic water-based paint. Try to keep the paint within the pencil lines. Wipe off any mistakes with a damp cloth before the paint dries. Let dry.

6 Paint the outer bands with copper metallic paint, using an artist's brush and even, fluid strokes. Leave to dry and protect by applying satin acrylic varnish with a household paintbrush.

# Craquelure stripes

### Materials and Equipment

Pale cream matt emulsion
  paint for the base coat
Two-part craquelure varnish
Ruler, pencil, masking tape
Artist's oil paints: green, pink
White spirit
Paint kettles
Household paintbrushes
Lint-free cloth
Matt oil varnish

Although craquelure varnish is most often used as an aging medium, it can have a contemporary style. This technique uses the effect as a textured background to hold colour. The addition of bright, contrasting colours gives an extra character to the decoration and helps the technique look less commonplace and more unusual.

1 *Apply the base coat and a craquelure effect (see Steps 1–4, page 121). Measure and mark up the surface into vertical bands.*

2 *Further detack masking tape by pressing the tacky side against a cotton or lint-free surface. Mask the lines marked in Step 1.*

3 *Dilute green artist's oil paint with enough white spirit to make a fluid wash. Gently brush the glaze onto the craquelure until it is held in the cracks. Repeat on alternate bands. Leave for one hour only.*

4 *Slightly dampen a cloth with white spirit and gently wipe over the surface to remove the top layer of colour, leaving the colour mostly in the cracks. Leave to dry completely.*

5 *Remove the masking tape and reapply to mask the newly painted strips.*

6 *Follow Steps 3–4 to apply dilute pink oil paint to the remaining stripes. Leave to dry. Remove the tape and protect by applying matt oil varnish with a household paintbrush.*

# Outline squares

## Materials and Equipment

Red matt emulsion paint for
  the base coat
Ruler, pencil, craft knife,
  cutting mat, masking tape
Manila stencil card
Metallic water-based paints:
  a selection of golds from
  dark to bright
Small paintbrushes
Decorator's sponge
Fine-grade wet-dry sandpaper
Beeswax
Lint-free cloth

Experimenting with a range of different brushstrokes and marks is an extremely simple way of achieving an individual finish that looks complicated. The edges of square masks and stencils are stippled, sponged and brushed with different shades of gold paint to outline shapes that intersect with each other. Do not overload the brushes and sponges or the light paint application will be difficult to control.

1 Apply the base coat. Sand the final dry coat well with fine-grade wet-dry sandpaper.

2 Mark squares of varying sizes on stencil card and cut them out with a sharp craft knife over a cutting mat. Keep the stencils and the masks.

3 Lightly fix the largest square stencil to the surface with masking tape. Load a small brush with dark gold metallic water-based paint and remove the excess. Stipple the paint around the inside edges of the stencil. Continue adding randomly spaced large squares. Leave to dry.

4 Attach a strip of tape rolled back on itself to the back of a square mask. Lightly fix the mask in position, overlapping one of the first gold squares. Dip a sponge in a little mid-gold paint and dab off the excess. Stipple the gold around the edge of the mask. Add more squares as desired and let dry.

5 Continue painting squares of decreasing size in different shades of gold. Use a brighter gold and try out another method of application, brushing the paint out from the centre.

6 Use the smallest square with the brightest gold, stippling it on with a small brush for another different effect. When you are happy with the arrangement, leave to dry and seal by applying beeswax with a lint-free cloth.

# Wallpaper

## Materials and Equipment

Quality lining paper
Matt emulsion paints: pale
  cream, cream
Rubber or foam stamps
Acrylic paints: such as green,
  orange, yellow, blue
Ruler, pencil
Household paintbrushes,
  fine artist's brush
Decorator's sponge
Matt acrylic glaze
Paint kettle

Making your own wallpaper is easier than you might imagine, and extremely cheap. Try to work with simple lines of decoration, even if these are not immediately obvious. Here, the first light leaf stamp is applied in regular vertical lines that are about the same distance apart. This acts as a helpful structural guide. The decoration chosen is best kept simple and limited. Use wallpaper paste as normal to fix it to the wall.

1 Use a brush to apply a coat of pale cream matt emulsion paint to quality lining paper. Leave to dry. Dampen a sponge and use this to apply a thin wash of cream matt emulsion paint all over. Let dry and repeat. Leave to dry.

2 Separate a square of the painted lining paper and use it to try out your stamps with various shades of acrylic paint. Aim to use pale colours with some stamps, to act as a background, and contrast these with other stamps in brighter colours.

3 Measure and lightly mark the repeats on the paper, working in vertical and horizontal bands but trying not to make the pattern too grid-like. Dampen a sponge and load the surface with a pale acrylic paint. Press the first stamp into the paint-pad sponge, then press it onto the paper. Repeat to give the first line of the pattern. Leave to dry.

4 For a different print, apply colour to the next stamp by touching the paint onto the stamp with a small piece of sponge. Use the stamp as before and repeat with another paint colour to form the next few lines of the pattern. Let dry.

5 Use the paint application method detailed in Step 4 to apply two colours to the stamp at one time. Repeat the stamping to complete the design.

6 Use a fine artist's brush to touch in the details. Let dry. Mix 3 parts matt acrylic glaze to 1 part water and coat the paper to protect it.

# Wallpaper border

## Materials and Equipment

Quality lining paper
Steel ruler, pencil, craft knife,
   cutting mat, masking tape
Matt emulsion paints: pale
   grey-green, mid-grey-green
Manila stencil card
Household paintbrushes
Decorator's sponge
Matt acrylic glaze

When creating your own wallpaper border you need some quality lining paper and a basic repeat stencil. It is best to use a large, simple repeat design rather than something narrow and detailed that may not be visible in a high position. This border is wider than the stencil because it features a painted line top and bottom to help the motif stand out. Use wallpaper paste as normal to fix it to the wall.

1 Use a craft knife and steel ruler over a cutting mat to cut lining-paper strips wide enough to house the stencil plus a painted line above and below.

2 Working on a flat surface, brush a coat of pale grey-green matt emulsion paint onto a paper strip. Leave to dry.

3 Make a large repeat stencil (see pages 218–219).

4 Measure and mark the border lines at the top and bottom of the strip. Use a small brush to paint in lines of mid-grey-green matt emulsion paint. Leave to dry. Use a sponge to stipple the edges of the border with the pale grey-green.

5 Lightly fix the stencil between the painted border lines with masking tape. Dip a sponge in mid-grey-green matt emulsion paint and dab off the excess. Stipple the colour through the stencil. Leave to dry – the lightly applied paint will dry quickly.

6 Stipple pale grey-green matt emulsion paint in the centre of the design, not going right up to the edges. The edges will be outlined in the darker grey-green for a three-dimensional effect. Realign the stencil and repeat Steps 5–6 to complete the border. Mix 3 parts matt acrylic glaze to 1 part water and coat the paper to protect it.

# Acrylic spatter and oil spray

## Materials and Equipment

Cream acrylic eggshell paint for
  the base coat
Acrylic paints: pale blue, brown
Artist's oil paints: raw sienna,
  raw umber
White spirit
Paint kettles
Household paintbrushes,
  nail brush
Plant sprays
Decorator's sponge
Hair dryer or hot-air gun
Ruler, pencil, masking tape
Dead flat oil varnish

This project combines oil- and water-based paints and
uses pump-handle plant spray guns as a quick and
easy way to apply a thin spattering of colour. The
loose, fluid wash that results is patinated with
spattered acrylic paint that acts as a resist to the next
spray of oil glaze. Practise spraying the oil glaze onto
newsprint until you are confident that the paint is
flowing well.

1 *Apply the base coat. Mix pale blue and brown acrylic paints each with a little water. Spatter the surface with dilute paints by dipping a brush in the paint and pulling back and releasing the bristles.*

2 *Mix equal amounts of raw sienna artist's oil paint and white spirit. Pour the glaze into a plant spray and, while the spattered paint is still wet, spray randomly all over. Let this layer of oil glaze settle then repeat with a raw umber oil glaze.*

3 *Spatter the acrylic colours again as in Step 1. This will misplace some of the oil glaze and add texture. Continue layering sprayed oil glazes and spattered acrylics until you are happy with the mix.*

4 *Speed up the drying process a little with a hair dryer or hot-air gun. Do not dry the paint completely.*

5 *Brush white spirit onto a sponge and lightly sponge the surface to lift off areas of oil paint and add more texturing. Dip a nail brush in the spirit and dab this on for a finer texture. Leave to dry.*

6 *Draw a line down the centre of the surface. Mask one side with masking tape. Brush the raw sienna oil glaze over one half and let dry. Reposition the tape and brush the other half with raw umber oil glaze. When dry, protect with dead flat oil varnish.*

# Simple freehand painting

## Materials and Equipment

Pale cream matt emulsion
   paint for the base coat
Lining paper, pencil, transfer
   paper, craft knife, cutting
   mat, masking tape, biro
Stencil acetate
Deep cream matt
   emulsion paint
Acrylic paints: burnt umber,
   raw umber, red
Paint kettles
Decorator's sponge
Artist's brush, household
   paintbrush
Foam roller head
Matt acrylic varnish

To someone with no drawing skills, the idea of using figurative imagery can be very daunting. However, by researching the kind of images you like from books and photographs, and sketching out ideas on lining paper first, the uninitiated artist can paint freehand motifs. Simple stencils cut for the repeat elements of the design could be enhanced with hand-painted details.

1 Apply the base coat. Dampen a sponge and use this to wash deep cream matt emulsion paint all over. Use a scrubbing motion to suggest an aged wall finish. Leave to dry.

2 Sketch out your design on a piece of lining paper until you are happy with the scale and layout.

3 Cut stencils of any repeat details (see Steps 2–3, page 213). You can use stencil acetate in the same way as stencil card, and, in this case, because it is easy to see through it is easier to place.

4 Place transfer paper between the lining-paper sketch and the surface and lightly fix in place with masking tape. Redraw the design with a biro to transfer it to the surface.

5 Mix a sepia paint from burnt umber, raw umber, and red acrylic paints. Dilute with water until fluid and slightly transparent. With an artist's brush, use long, smooth brushstrokes to paint in the lines. Paint sepia leaves and reapply the paint to those areas of the design in shadow. Let dry.

6 Lightly fix the detail stencils in position with tape. Dip a foam roller head in red acrylic paint mixed with a touch of raw umber and remove the excess. Stipple the paint through the stencils and let dry. Protect with matt acrylic varnish.

# Grisaille

## Materials and Equipment

Ruler, pencil, tracing paper,
   transfer paper, masking tape
Matt emulsion paints: grey,
   white
Black acrylic paint
Paint kettles
Artist's brushes, household
   paintbrush
Fine-grade wet-dry sandpaper
Matt acrylic varnish

The grisaille painting style was traditionally used to imitate plaster or painted-wood relief work. The monochrome finish can be achieved using just three tones of a single colour. It is usually easiest to begin with the mid-tone across the whole surface and then add the lighter and darker tones to touch in the foreground and distant planes. Decide on the light source and experiment on paper before you commit.

1 *Decide on your design and enlarge photocopies to fit the area you wish to decorate. Mix grey matt emulsion paint with varying degrees of white matt emulsion paint or black acrylic paint to create three tones, dark grey, mid-grey and light grey.*

2 *Trace the outline and details of the design from the photocopies. Experiment with washes of colour on the photocopies to decide on the tonal range you will be using and to ascertain the source of light you will be working with.*

3 *Apply a base coat of mid-grey and sand with fine-grade wet-dry sandpaper.*

4 *Place transfer paper between the tracing-paper sketch and the surface and lightly fix in place with masking tape. Redraw the design to transfer it.*

5 *Use masking tape to mask a border around the transferred design. Start with the darkest grey, using an artist's brush to paint it into the background, from the tape to the outline of the mid-grey main shape. Add the dark grey details, referring to the experimental colour work done in Step 2. Let dry.*

6 *Paint the highlight areas with the lightest grey. Let dry, then rework any of the mid-tone and dark areas as necessary. Leave to dry then protect by applying matt acrylic varnish with a household paintbrush.*

# Decoupage grisaille

## Materials and Equipment

Ruler, pencil, sharp scissors
Pale cream matt
    emulsion paint
Burnt umber acrylic paint
Paint kettles
Household paintbrushes,
    long-bristled artist's brushes
Decorator's sponges
PVA or white glue
Matt acrylic varnish

An alternative to the painted tradition, this is a quick-and-easy way to imitate a solid, carved decoration. Three tones of a single colour – dilute washes of light, mid-, and dark brown – are applied to a paper motif that is stuck in position to suggest a three-dimensional stone relief. Adding a painted shadow line around the stuck-on paper has enhanced the relief effect.

1 *Mix burnt umber acrylic paint with varying degrees of pale cream matt emulsion paint to create three tones, dark brown, mid-brown and light brown. Use sponges to thickly stipple on patches of each brown, overlapping in places to blend the colours. Leave to dry.*

2 *Photocopy the chosen design and enlarge to the required size. Make marks on the surface to help you align each separate element later.*

3 *Dilute 1 part mid-brown paint with 3 parts water and use a brush to wash the glaze all over the paper copies. Leave to dry.*

4 *Dilute the light and dark browns as in Step 3. Decide on the source of light, then use a long-bristled artist's brush to paint in the highlights and shadows to give a three-dimensional feel. Let dry.*

5 *Carefully cut out the design using sharp scissors. Use PVA or white glue to stick down the paper elements, following the pencil marks made in Step 2. Gently wipe a damp sponge over the paper to remove any air bubbles. When the glue is dry, wash off the pencil marks with a damp sponge.*

6 *Use the mid-brown to paint a thin shadow line around the paper cut-out. Using the long-bristled artist's brush will help keep the line constant and even. Protect with matt acrylic varnish.*

# Glossary

**acrylics** Fast-drying, water-based paints.

**ageing** Variety of techniques for simulating the effect of time and wear on new paint, wood or plasterwork.

**base coat** First coat of paint for most decorative paint finishes, applied before the glaze or ground coat.

**binder** Paint ingredient that binds the particles together.

**blending brush** *see* **softening brush**

**bole** Coloured clay mixed with animal-skin glue, sometimes applied over gesso before gilding.

**border** Design around the edge of panel, wall or floor. It may be stenciled, printed or painted freehand.

**bravura** Spirited brushwork.

**buff** To polish with a cloth.

**burnisher** Extremely smooth agate polisher used in water-gilding.

**casein** Quick-drying, milk-based paint that can be varnished.

**clay plaster** Versatile, natural 'breathing' material.

**collage** Work put together from assembled fragments of materials such as paper and fabrics.

**colourwashing** Simple water-based paint technique used to produce a softly textured, patchy finish achieved by applying several layers of thin paint.

**combing** Technique in which the teeth of a decorator's comb are scraped through a surface glaze to reveal the colour below.

**complementary colours** Any pair of colours that, when placed on a colour wheel, occupy opposing positions. The complementary of any primary colour (red, yellow, blue) is the secondary colour made by mixing the other two.

**crackleglaze** *see* **craquelure**

**craquelure** Decorative glaze developed in eighteenth-century France to reproduce the fine network of cracks on Eastern lacquerwork and pottery. Also known as crackleglaze.

**cross-hatching** Two sets of parallel lines, one on top of the other, with the second set at an angle to the first.

**decoupage** Method of decorating walls and objects with paper cut-outs protected by a clear glaze or varnish.

**distemper** Group of paints formed by mixing pigments with water, bound with casein, glue or egg, which were widely used before the introduction of emulsion paints.

**distressing** Process of artificially abrading a new surface to create the appearance of age.

**dragging** Technique of pulling a long-haired brush through wet transparent glaze or distemper to produce a series of fine lines.

**dry-brushing** Paint technique that keeps the bristle surface of a brush relatively dry in order to build up a cloudy effect, or to touch up the highlights of a textured surface.

**drywall** Plaster substitute such as plasterboard.

**Dutch metal leaf** Imitation gold or silver used in gilding.

**eggshell** Mid-sheen, oil- or acrylic-based paint used as a base coat for basic and bravura finishes. White eggshell is also used for mixing some pale colours for the glaze coat. Also used to describe a mid-sheen finish of paints and varnishes.

**emulsion** Water-based paint, suitable for most decorative paint finishes if protected with a glaze or varnish.

**faux effects** Literally: 'false' effects. That is, finishes created to imitate another material, such as marble (*faux marbre*) or wood (*faux bois*).

**fitch** Hog-hair brush suitable for oil work (one type is available for watercolour work). The five types are round, filbert, long, short and herkomer. Used in many techniques and sometimes as an alternative to a household brush.

**flat finish** Matt, non-glossy finish.

**flogging** Coloured glaze is laid over a base coat, then flogged with a long-bristled brush. This gives a mottled effect.

**flogging brush** Coarse horsehair brush used for dragging and flogging; available in a range of sizes.

**frottage** Literally: 'rubbing' (from the French *frotter* – to rub). A technique involving rubbing newsprint over a wet glaze or rubbing a loaded paintbrush on a dry surface.

**gesso** Fine plaster traditionally prepared with rabbit-skin glue and whiting, and applied to surfaces in many layers to give a completely smooth finish before gilding or painting. Also now available in a ready-mixed, substitute form.

**gilding** Method of giving surfaces a metallic finish by the application of metal leaf or paint.

**glaze** Any paint that has been diluted and in which colour can be mixed.

**gold leaf** Sheets of gold beaten to a wafer thinness used in gilding.

**grisaille** Visual trick that harnesses monochrome shades of paint to represent areas of light and shade and thus create, on a flat surface, the illusion of a three-dimensional ornament or an architectural feature.

**heartgrainer** Comb that produces faux woodgrain effects.

**hog-hair brush** Tough, springy hog-hair brush that is suitable for acrylic- and oil-painting.

**lacquering** Technique for simulating the high-gloss finish of Chinese and Japanese lacquer.

**limewash** Substance made of slaked lime and water used to whiten exterior walls. Also known as whitewash.

**lining** Technique for outlining the shape of a surface with one or more decorative lines.

**lining paper** Plain, flat wallpaper used to line the walls of a room, often over imperfect plaster. It can be painted if first sealed with diluted undercoat.

**luminosity** Measure of brightness of a paint.

**masking** Covering a surface to provide a barrier against a layer of paint.

**masking tape** Used to mask out areas, hold on stencils etc.

**methylated spirits** Industrial alcohol used as a solvent.

**mica** Rock-forming mineral, such as slate, which crystallises into easily separated layers.

**Mondrian, Piet** (1872–1944) Dutch abstract painter who limited himself to rectangular forms and very few colours.

**muslin** Fine, woven cotton fabric used for curtains, hangings, etc

**oil gilding** Technique in which transfer gold is applied to a surface.

**oil glaze** *see* **glaze**

**oxidation** Chemical reaction of a material with oxygen in the air.

**painter's tape** Low-tack masking tape

**patina** Colour and texture that appear on the surface of a material as a result of age or atmospheric corrosion.

**patination** Artificially created patina.

**pigment** Colouring matter used in paints.

**plumbline** Weighted string used for marking verticals.

**primary colours** Colours from which all others can be mixed. The primary colours in paint are red, yellow and blue.

**primer** Sealant for new plaster or woodwork before painting.

**ragging** Paint technique that employs a crumpled piece of rag to create decorative broken-colour finishes.

**roller** Tool with a revolving cylinder covered in various materials and used for applying paint.

**sable brush** Good-quality paintbrush.

**sandpaper** Abrasive paper available in varying degrees of coarseness. *See* **wet-dry sandpaper**.

**secondary colours** Colours made by mixing two primary colours.

**shellac** Resin in thin plates.

**softening brush** Long-haired brush used for softening and blending paint in marbling, woodgraining and many other bravura finishes. Badger hair softeners are easier to use but more expensive than hog-hair softeners. Available in a range of sizes.

**solvent** Part of oil-based paints that evaporates during drying.

**spirit dyes** Used to simulate a distressed surface.

**sponging** Paint technique that uses a damp sponge to produce a mottled, patchy effect.

**spraying** Method of directing paint onto a surface in a fine spray.

**stainers** Sometimes known as universal stainers. Used as an alternative to artist's oil paints for colouring glaze. The range of colours is less extensive and less subtle than artist's oils. *See* **tinter**.

**stencil brush** Short-haired brushes designed to hold small amounts of paint for stencilling. Available in a wide range of sizes and with long or short handles.

**stencil card** Stout oiled manila card, from which shapes are cut in order to make stencils.

**stencilling** Method of decoration in which paint is applied through a cut-out design to create images on a surface.

**stippling** Painting or texturing a surface with a fine, mottled pattern, using a stippler or stiff-bristled brush.

**stippling brush** Rectangular brush used for a stippled finish and for removing excess paint in cornices and architraves etc. Available in a variety of sizes.

**stucco** Fine plaster-type material used both to cover exterior brickwork and to decorate internal walls and ceilings.

**sugar soap** Alkaline degreasing agent: a type of cleaner that can be applied to a surface before work starts. It needs to be thoroughly rinsed afterwards.

**tertiary colours** Colours made by mixing two secondary colours.

**tinter** Also known as universal tinter. Highly concentrated colouring agent. *See* **stainer**.

**tone** Term used to describe how dark or light a colour is. Different colours may be the same tone.

**tongue-and-groove** Joint made between two boards by means of a tongue projecting from the edge of one board that slots into a groove along the edge of the other.

**transfer leaf** Sheets of gold or silver leaf attached to tissue paper used in oil gilding.

**trompe l'oeil** Any of a variety of optical illusions, such as *grisaille*, that are designed, literally, to 'trick the eye'.

**undercoat** Matt paint applied to a surface before the base coat.

**universal stainer** *see* **stainer**.

**universal tinter** *see* **tinter**.

**varnish** Transparent protective coat applied to completed paint finishes. Varnishes may be matt, eggshell or gloss, and they may be water-, oil-, or spirit-based.

**veining** Specialist technique for painting the veins on simulated marble.

**water-gilding** Technique for applying transfer or loose leaf to a surface.

**wet-dry sandpaper** Abrasive paper that may be used with water to achieve a really smooth finish.

**whitewash** *see* **limewash**

**whiting** Finely ground calcium carbonate used in making gesso.

**woodgraining** Technique used to imitate the characteristic markings of a variety of natural woodgrains.

# Index

Figures in *italics* indicate captions.

## A

acrylic eggshell paint 17
acrylic primer 17, 19
acrylic spatter and oil spray 244–5
adhesives 20, *20*
alkyd paints *see* oil-based paints 16
antiquing with coloured waxes 150–51
artist's acrylic paint 18
artist's oil paints 18, *18*, 19

## B

basic techniques 26–33
beeswax *20*, 21, 33, 63, 79, 97
binders 12, 13, 16, 188
bird's-eye maple effect 142–3
bole 19, 190–91, 192–3, 212
Breccia marble 130–31
bronze powders 19, 169, 188–9
brushes 22–3, *22, 23*, 28–30, *30–31*
building up colours 216–17
button polish 21

## C

Carrara marble 132–3
casein 17, 56, 57
circles 234–5
clay plastering 18, 85, 108–9
clouds, fake 48–9
collage *6, 41*, 122–3, 124–5
colour stainer (tinter) 16
colour theory 8–15
colourwashing *6*, 13, 17, 71, 75, 83
combing 114–15, 138, 139
combs 24, *24*
complementary colours 10, *11*
copper loose leaf 18, 196–7
crackle effect 118–19
crackle medium 19
crackleglaze (craquelure) *6*, 19, 85,
    120–21, 236–7
cross-hatching 46, 47, 57

## D

decorative paper 85
decorator's plaster (gypsum) 18
decoupage *6, 15*, 121, 124–5, 250-51

denim effect 100–101
distemper 12
distressing with spirit dyes 206–7
dragging 29, *29*, 60–61, 81, 87, 89,
    101, 103, 138, 139, 154–5
dry-brushing 29, *29*, 54–5, 57
dusting 87
Dutch leaf 18, 194–5

## E

emulsion paint 16, 17
exterior house paint 18

## F

fabric effects *see* leather and
    fabric effects
fabric patterning 78–9
feathers 24, *24*
floating marble effect 166–7
flogging 29, *29*, 138, 139
found-material printing 226–7
freehand painting 246–7
French polish 21
frottage 82–3, 228–9
fruitwood effect 144–5, 153

## G

gesso 85, 19, 112–13, 127, 128, 190,
    192, 193, 195
gilding *6*, 169
    on glass 198–9
    oil gilding with real silver 192–3
    water gilding with real gold 190–91
glaze 16, 17
glossary 252–3
gold leaf 18, 190–91
gold-painted squares 174–5
graining 102
granite effect 136–7
grisaille 248–9, 250–251
gypsum 18

## H

health and safety 34
heart grainers 24, *24*

## I

imitation gold and silver transfer leaf
    194–5
inspiration boards *15*

iridescent/opalescent washes 184–5
iron effect, rusted 178–9

## K

knives 24, *24*, 25, *25*
knotting solution 20, 21

## L

lace stencil 80–81
lacquer effect 62–3
lapis lazuli effect 162–3
leather and fabric effects 96–105
limestone paving effect 94–5
limewashing 12
linen effect 60–61
lining 6, 30, *30*
lining-paper bands 232–3
linseed oil 20, *20*
loose leaf 18
luster paints, mixing 186–7

## M

mahogany effect 146–7
malachite effect 164–5
marbling 127, 128–37
marmorino plaster 18
masking 28, *28*
masking tape 25, *25*
materials and equipment 16–25
matt paints, and metallic paints 172–3
medium 16
metal leaf 18, 19, 169, 188, 204
    metallic paint and 200–201
    oil and water on 202–3
metallic effects 168–209
metallic paint 17, 169, 170–71
    and matte paints 172–3
    and metal leaf 200–201
    patination 204–5
metallic powders 19
methylated spirit *20*
mica 19, 85, 116
moiré silk, imitation 102–3
Mondrian style 66–7
mood/colour boards *12*, 13–15
mural 220–21
muslin frottage 82–3

## O

oak effect 138–9
oil gilding with real silver 192–3
oil spray, acrylic spatter and 244–5
oil and water on metal leaf 202–3
oil-based (alkyd) paints 16, 17, 127
opalescent and iridescent washes
  184–5
opalescent solid colour 182–3
outline squares 238–9
overlaying colours 76–7

## P

paint effects selector 35–40
  metallic effects 39
  patterns and motifs 40
  textured effects 37
  traditional effects 38
  working with colour 36
paint stripper 20, 20, 27, 27
paint-to-glaze mix 70
painter's tape 25, 25, 28, 28
paints
  ingredients 16
  make your own 56–7
  mixing 28, 28
  types of paint 16–18
parquet floor, fake 156–7
patination 169, 204–5, 208–9
patterning 212–13, 214–15
patterns and motifs 210–51
peeling paint effect 148–9
pigments 12, 13, 16, 18
pine effect 140–41
plaster effects 106–13
plasterer's hawk and float 24, 24
plastering 13
  aged plaster effect 110–11
plasters 18
plumb-bob, plumbline 25, 25
porphyry effect 158–9
primary colours 9, 9
priming your surface 27
printing blocks 222–3
PVA see white glue

## R

rabbit-skin size 19
ragging 74–5
repeats

found-material printing 226–7
frottage 228–9
  printing blocks 222–3
  sprayed leaves and cutouts 230–31
  vegetable stamps 224–5
rhodocrosite effect 134–5
roller use
  cleaning 31
  loading 31, 31
  Mondrian style 66–7
  patterning 70–71
  spots 72–3
  transparent stripes 64–5
rollers 23, 23
rusted iron effect 178–9

## S

safety 34, 34
sandpaper 25, 25, 26, 26
sandstone effect 86–7
secondary colours 9, 9
shellac 20, 21, 21, 33, 33
Sienna marble 128–9
silver leaf 18, 192–3, 194, 195, 198,
  199
slate, fake 85, 88–9
snakeskin, imitation 98–9
softening 30, 30
solvents 13, 20, 20
spirit dyes, distressing with 206–7
sponges 23, 23, 32, 32
spray adhesive 20
spray paint 81
  and fabric patterning 78–9
sprayed leaves and cutouts 230–31
squares 174–5, 238–9
steel effect 176–7
stencil card 25, 25
stencil paint 17, 18
stenciling 6, 80–81, 98–9, 175, 212
  building up colours 216–17
  with filler and mica 116–17
  freehand painting 246–7
  irregular patterning 212–13
  making a repeat stencil 218–19
  regular patterning 214–15
  simple mural 220–21
  wallpaper border 242–3
stippling 29, 29, 65, 87, 95, 99, 102
  and colour wash 52–3

drag and stipple with lining 154–5
  fade 58–9
stone blockwork, mock 92–3
stone effects 86–95
stripes 64–5, 68–9
stucco 18, 106–7, 213
suede, imitation 85, 104–5
sugar soap 26
surface
  preparation 26–7
  priming 27
  rough/smooth 11 .

## T

terracotta technique 90–91
tertiary colours 9, 9
textured paints and plasters 18
textured wall finish 18, 91, 95
thinners 20, 20
tinter (colour stainer) 16
tints 10, 10
tone 10
tortoiseshell effect 160–61
transfer leaf 18
trompe l'oeil 152–3
turpentine, pure 20, 20

## U

undercoat, oil-based 17
universal stainer (tinter) 18

## V

varnish 21, 21, 63, 80, 85, 88
  applying 33, 33
vegetable stamps 224–5
verdigris effect 180–81

## W

wallpaper 240–41
  border 242–3
warm/cool colours 11, 11
water gilding with real gold 190–91
water-based paint 16
waxes 20–21, 20
  antiquing with coloured waxes 150–51
wet-dry sandpaper 25, 25
white glue 20, 27, 27, 80
white spirit 20, 20
wood effects 138–47
wood paint 17

# Resources

Many of the tools and materials used in this book can be found at hardware and fine-art stores. Check the yellow pages for the location nearest you. Otherwise, you can contact any of the following suppliers:

## USA

**Dover Publications**
11 East Ninth Avenue
New York, NY 10019
www.doverpublications.com

**Homestead House Authentic Milk Paint**
95 Niagara Street
Toronto, ON M5V 1C3
Tel (416) 504-9984

**Lee Valley Tools Ltd.**
PO Box 6295, Station J
Ottawa, ON Canada K2A 1TA
Toll-Free 1-800-267-8767
Toll-Free Fax 1-800-668-1807

**Paint Effects**
2426 Fillmore Street
San Francisco, CA 94115
www.painteffects.com

**Pierre Finkelstein Institute of Decorative Painting, Inc.**
20 West 20th Street, Suite 1009
New York, NY 10011
www.pfinkelstein.com

**Pratt & Lambert Inc.**
PO Box 22
Buffalo, NY 14240
www.prattandlambert.com

**R&F Handmade Paints, Inc.**
110 Prince Street
Kingston, NY 12401
www.rfpaints.com

**Sepp Leaf Products, Inc.**
381 Park Avenue South
New York, NY 10016
www.seppleaf.com

**The Texston Company**
www.texston.com

**Woodcrafter's Supply Corp.**
www.woodcraft.com

**The Old Fashioned Milk Paint Co.**
www.milkpaint.com

**Absolute Coatings Inc.**
www.lastnlast.com

**Adele Bishop**
www.adelebishop.com

## UK

**Craig & Rose plc**
172 Leith Walk
Edinburgh EH6 5EB
www.craigandrose.com

**Dulux Decorating Centre**
89 Richford Street
London W6 7HJ
www.dulux.co.uk

**Leyland SDM**
43-45 Farringdon Road
London EC1
www.leyland.co.uk

**Daler-Rowney Ltd.**
12 Percy Street
London W1A 2BP
www.daler-rowney.com

**W.Habberley Meadows**
5 Saxon Way
Chelmsley Wood
Birmingham B37 5AY
www.habberleymeadows.co.uk

## AUSTRALIA

**Porter's Original Paints**
Sydney, Australia
Tel (818) 623-9394
Fax (818) 623-9210
www.porters.com.au

# Acknowledgements

The book is dedicated to baby Jessie, the best companion during much of the work, and Stephen for all his support.

I would like to thank the following people for their hard work and help with the production of this book: John Hilborne, Matt Watson, Louisa Swan, and particularly Sarah Davies who assisted and inspired me. A special mention for Tilly, Amber, Lutia, and Neave for their beautiful boards.

For their generosity and support for this project and for supplying products and advice, I would like to thank: Neil from Natural Building Technologies Ltd, Cholsey Grange, Ibstone, High Wycombe, Bucks HP14 3XT, e-mail: www.natural-building.co.uk; Stuart R. Stevenson, 68 Clerkenwell Road, London E3; Tim France for patiently working on to complete a book of many pictures and for great baby entertaining!

I particularly wish to breathe a group sigh of relief with all at Quarto, the project is complete, thank you.